Science Panorama 7

Chemistry

Series Editor
Lipika Dutta

Collins

Science Panorama 7

Chemistry

Series Editor

Lipika Dutta

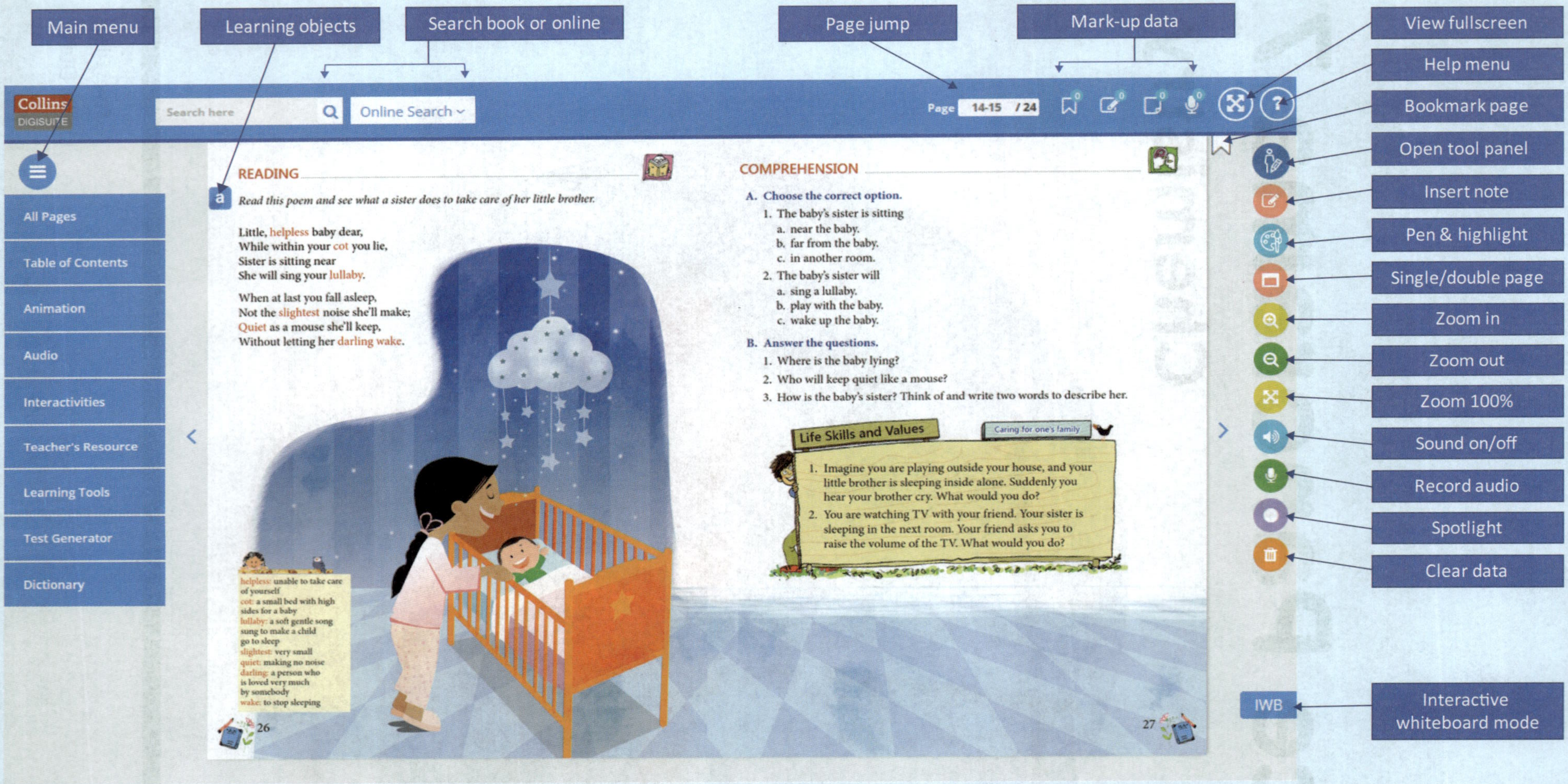

Student + Teacher		Teacher-only
a animations	**ia** activities	**lp** lesson plans
ilt instructor-led tutorials	**w** worksheets	**w** worksheets
g games	audio	**tn** teacher's notes
v videos		**ak** answer keys

Preface

Science Panorama is a series of books for Classes 1 to 8, which includes 3 books each for Physics, Chemistry and Biology for middle school. The middle school series has been updated based on the **new syllabus** prescribed by the **Council for the Indian School Certificate Examinations**. In line with the new syllabus, a thematic, coherent and structured approach has been followed and all the new topics suggested in the syllabus have been included. Chapter-wise worksheets have also been provided to effectively integrate subject knowledge and life skills for overall development.

This updated edition also emphasizes on developing scientific skills such as observation, investigation, analysis, research and other inferential skills. It focuses on development of concepts as well as their application in real life. Sufficient examples from everyday life have been provided to help learners understand the concepts using age-appropriate language. Colourful illustrations and well-labelled diagrams have been included to engage learners and aid their understanding.

Some Key Features

Science in Context: Additional information on the topic being taught

Do You Know? Interesting facts related to the given topic

Challenge Yourself: Questions testing students' ability to reason and extrapolate

Activities: Individual/collaborative activities to hone experimental and deduction skills

Know the Scientist: Famous scientists and their contribution to the topic at hand

Greenathon: Some tips to keep the environment clean and green

Revision Zone: In-text questions for assessing progress in the course of learning

Keywords: Important terms from the chapter along with their definitions

In a Nutshell: Summary of the chapter content

Exercise: Variety of questions given at the end of each chapter

Subject Integration Worksheets: To effectively integrate knowledge across subjects

Life Skills Worksheets: To create awareness, empathy and a positive attitude towards self and others

Assessment papers: Two assessment papers at the end of the book for effective evaluation

We would like to take this opportunity to thank all the teachers who reviewed the books and provided their valuable feedback, which helped in improving the quality of the content.

Any suggestions or constructive criticism from the users are welcome. We shall try to incorporate those in the future editions.

Authors

Key Features

Do You Know?

Interesting facts related to the given topic

Do You Know?

Pieces of pumice rocks can float on water. This is because the air pores in them make the stone less dense than water. This helps [the] stone to float for a [whi]le after a wh[ile]

Science in Context

In a liquid and a gas, the molecules are loosely packed, so they have some regions with more molecules and other regions with fewer molecules. The movement [o]f molecules from a region [of h]igher concentration to [a] lower con[centration]

Science in Context

Additional information on the topic being taught

Challenge Yourself

Questions testing students' ability to reason and extrapolate

Challenge Yourself

You might have noticed that cut pieces of some vegetables and fruits like potato, apple, etc., turn brown when exposed to air if they are not consumed immediately. [Do] you know what kind of a [change] it is?

Know the Scientist

Joseph Priestley (1733–1804) was an English chemist. He is credited for the isolation and discovery of oxygen in its gaseous state. He named it as 'dephlogisticated air'. He also synthesized nitrous oxide (laughing gas).

Know the Scientist

Famous scientists and their contribution to the topic at hand

Activity 1

Aim: To study that matter has mass

Materials required: Two paper bags, some marbles and a weighing balance

Procedure:

1. Weigh the two empty paper bags using a weighing balance.
2. Now add some marbles to one of the paper bags.

Observation: The paper bag that is fille
arbles becomes heavier when com
mpty one.

Activity

To hone experimental and deduction skills

Revision Zone

In-text questions for assessing progress

Revision Zone

Give one word for each of the following.

1. The substance formed when two or mo atoms are bound together ________
2. The pure substance that contains only kind of atoms ________
3. The number of atoms present in a mol of an element ________
4. The chemical formula of ammonia ________

Keywords

Pure substance: a substance that consists of only one kir

Mixture: a substance that contains two or more different

Winnowing: a method that uses the action of wind to sepa a mixture

Sieving: a method that uses a sieve to separate undesirabl

Filtration: the process of using a porous medium (filter) to s particles suspended in a liquid

Distillation: the method of separation of components of and condensation

Centrifugation: the process of separation of fine, inso using a centrifuge

tional distillation: the process of separation ference in their boiling points

Keywords

Definitions of key terms from the chapter

Exercise

Variety of questions given at the end of each chapter

ose the odd one out. Give reasons for the choice.

a. Carbon, gold, copper, aluminium
b. Chlorine, sulphur, germanium, iodine
c. Silver, water, zinc, calcium
d. O, C, Au, Mg
e. N, ZnO, H, Cd

7. **Differentiate between the following.**

a. Melting and freezing
b. Vaporization and condensation
c. Elements and compounds
d. Metals and non-metals
e. An atom and a molecule

8. **Give reasons for the following.**

Solids are hard and rigid.
ids take the shape of

Worksheet

Subject Integration

Identify the preservative methods that are suitable for the food items given below.

Food item	Preservation method used	Reason for selecting the metho
Milk		
Fish		
Pulses		
Meat		
Fruits		

Worksheet

Thematic worksheets on integration of knowledge across subjects and Life Skills

Contents

Matter and Its Composition

1

What I shall learn

- Properties of matter
- Composition of matter
- States of matter

Introduction

All the things around us are made up of matter. Right from the food we eat, the water we drink, the chair we sit on, the books we read to the air we breathe, everything is made of matter. Even we, human beings, are made of matter. All the things mentioned above have mass and occupy a certain space. Therefore, **matter** can be defined as anything that has mass and occupies space.

Let us learn about the properties of matter and different states of matter in detail in this chapter.

Properties of Matter

Matter has the following properties.

- **Matter has mass**: When we carry an empty basket, it feels very light. When we fill the basket with books, toys and clothes, we find the basket a little heavy. This is because matter has mass. Let us do an activity to understand this concept.

Activity 1

Aim: To study that matter has mass

Materials required: Two paper bags, some marbles and a weighing balance

Procedure:

1. Weigh the two empty paper bags using a weighing balance.
2. Now add some marbles to one of the paper bags.

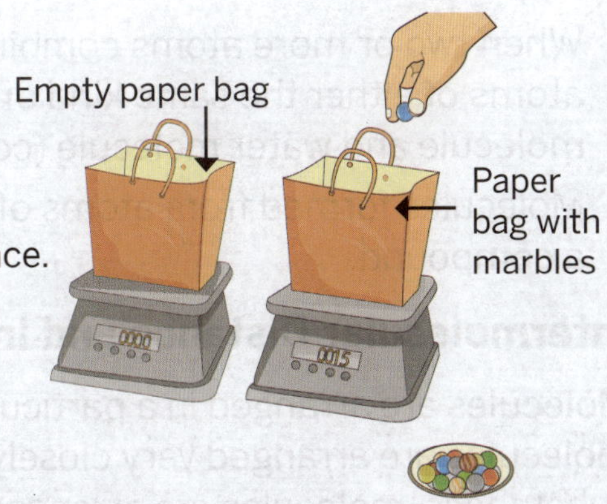

Observation: The paper bag that is filled with marbles becomes heavier when compared to the empty one.

Conclusion: Matter has mass.

- **Matter occupies space**: Take a deflated balloon and blow air into it. Air fills up the balloon. Now, try to fill air in an already blown-up balloon. Can we fill the same amount of air in this

▲ Air fills up the balloon

balloon also? No, because some air is already occupying space inside the balloon. In other words, matter occupies space. Similarly, our books occupy space in our bag. Our lunch occupies space in our lunch box. Let us do an activity to know about this concept.

Activity 2

Aim: To study that matter occupies space

Materials required: Beaker, stone and water

Procedure:

1. Fill the beaker with water up to the brim.
2. Now, gently drop the stone into the beaker. The stone should be dropped from a reasonable height such that the beaker does not break.

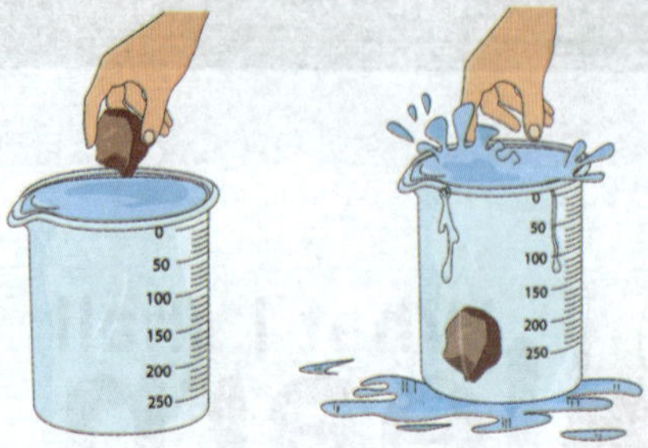

Observation: The water spills over the beaker.

Conclusion: Water occupies the space in the beaker. When the stone is dropped, the water spills over the beaker to make room for the stone. Thus, we can conclude that matter occupies space.

Composition of Matter

When people build walls and other structures using bricks, they place the bricks one over the other and add cement to bind the bricks. We can say that bricks are the building blocks of walls, houses and other buildings. A brick helps to make buildings, but what is a brick made of? To find out, break a brick into pieces. When we break it completely, we get a fine powder. Is a small grain of that powder, the smallest unit of a brick? No, the brick is made up of particles that are smaller than even a grain of powder.

The smallest particle that makes up a substance or matter is called an **atom**.

- An atom is the basic unit of an **element**, which represents a substance. Examples of elements are hydrogen, oxygen, gold and silver. Atoms retain the properties of their respective elements.
- When two or more atoms combine, they form a **molecule**. Molecules are made up of atoms of either the same kind or different kinds. Examples of molecules include hydrogen molecule and water molecule (containing both hydrogen atom and oxygen atom).
- Molecules formed from atoms of different kinds are called **compounds**. Water is a compound.

Intermolecular Distance and Intermolecular Force

Molecules are arranged in a particular manner in each substance. In some substances, molecules are arranged very closely with very less space between them and in some other substances, molecules are arranged far apart. The distance between the molecules of a substance is called **intermolecular distance**.

The molecules in a substance are held together by a force called **intermolecular force**. The stronger the intermolecular force, the closer are the molecules and the shorter is the intermolecular distance.

States of Matter

When we observe our surroundings, we find that matter exists in different forms. Matter exists in three different states—solids, liquids and gases. But, what determines whether a substance exists in a solid, liquid or gaseous state? The existence of a substance in a particular state is determined by the properties of matter, which include the intermolecular force of attraction between the molecules. Some of these properties can be altered by a change in pressure or temperature.

Let us consider the example of water. Water exists in liquid state at room temperature. When we boil water at 100°C, it converts into steam, that is, its gaseous state. When liquid water is cooled to 0°C, it converts into ice, that is, its solid state. The figure given alongside shows the three states of water. Let us learn more about each state of matter.

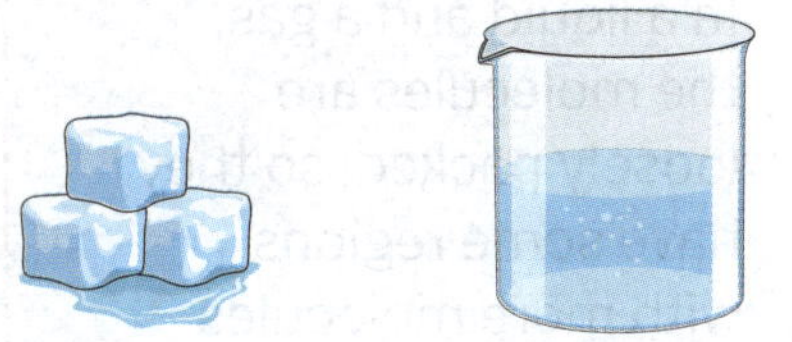

(a) Ice (solid) (b) Water (liquid)

(c) Steam (gas)

▲ Three states of water

Solids

Observe the image of the chair given alongside. Does it have a definite shape? Yes, it has a definite shape. Even if we move it from one place to another, its shape remains the same. Also, it has a definite volume that never changes. A substance with a definite shape and volume is called a **solid**.

▲ A solid substance has a definite shape and volume

Solids are mostly hard and rigid. Due to this reason, it is not easy to compress solids. Solids have a fixed boundary, shape and volume. We can change the shape of some solids by applying force, but their volume will remain the same. For example, the shape of solids like a sponge changes when we compress them.

Arrangement of Molecules in Solids

In solids, the molecules are closely packed. This is because the intermolecular force between the molecules of solids is strong. Therefore, molecules are not free to move around. This is the reason behind the fixed shape of solids.

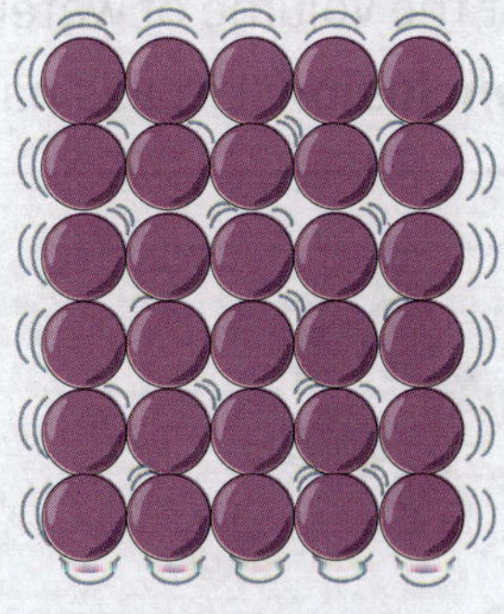

▲ Arrangement of molecules in solids

Properties of Solids

- The molecules in a solid are tightly packed.
- Solids have a definite shape and volume.
- Solids are hard and rigid.
- Solids are not easily compressible.
- Solids do not diffuse.

Science in Context

In a liquid and a gas, the molecules are loosely packed, so they have some regions with more molecules and other regions with fewer molecules. The movement of molecules from a region of higher concentration to a region of lower concentration is called **diffusion**. The movement of molecules continues until there is equal distribution in the medium. Diffusion allows molecules to spread out and mix with other molecules.

Liquids

We have learned that solids have a definite shape and size. What about liquids? What is the shape of a liquid? Take a conical flask and a beaker. Pour some water into the beaker first. Note the shape of the water. We can see that it takes the shape of the beaker. Now, pour the same amount of water into the conical flask. The water takes the shape of the conical flask. This means that water or any other liquid, in general, does not have a definite shape. It takes the shape of the container it is kept in. The amount of water in both the containers is the same. This means that water has a fixed or definite volume though its shape varies. A substance that has a definite volume but not a definite shape is called a **liquid**.

The shape of a liquid changes from container to container. This indicates that a liquid is not hard and rigid like a solid. A liquid is compressible to some extent, since the intermolecular distance in liquids is more than that in solids. Liquids have the ability to flow which makes them diffuse from one region to another. For example, if we put a drop of ink into a glass of water, it spreads uniformly and the water turns blue.

Activity 3

Aim: To understand that liquids have a definite volume but not a definite shape

Materials required: Glass bowl, glass tumbler, glass jug and water

Procedure:

1. Fill 50 mℓ water into the glass tumbler.
2. Observe the shape of the water.
3. Transfer the water into the bowl and observe the shape of the water.
4. Similarly, transfer the water into the jug and then observe the shape of the water.

A liquid takes the shape of the container it is stored in

Observation: The shape of water changes according to the shape of the vessel it is poured into, but the volume of water remains the same.

Conclusion: Liquids have a definite volume but not a definite shape.

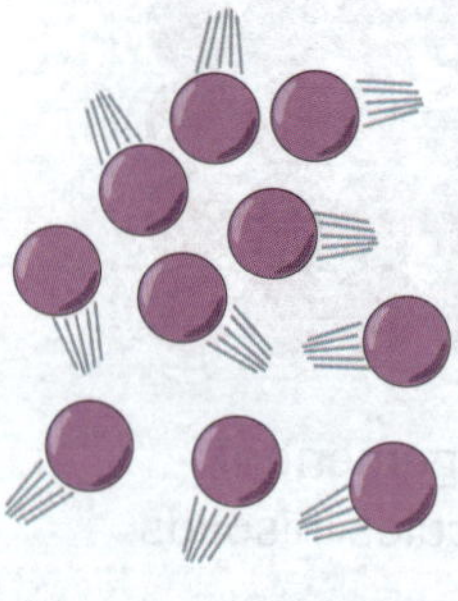

▲ Arrangement of molecules in liquids

Arrangement of Molecules in Liquids

Liquids have a weaker intermolecular force between their molecules than solids. So, their intermolecular distance is more than that in solids. In other words, the molecules in liquids are less closely packed than in solids. Therefore, liquids are not rigid and hard like solids. The molecules in a liquid are loosely bound and can move around easily. This is the reason why liquids can flow.

Properties of Liquids

- In liquids, the molecules are loosely packed.
- Liquids do not have a definite shape but have a definite volume.
- Liquids are compressible unlike the solids.
- Liquids diffuse slowly.
- Liquids flow from a higher level to a lower level.

Gases

When we fill a cycle tyre or a balloon with air, the gas (air) takes the shape and volume of the tyre and the balloon, respectively. This means that gases do not have a fixed shape.

Take a balloon and fill it with air. Then, prick the balloon to burst it. What happens to the air in it? We feel the air move out in all directions. This means that gases can move freely in all directions. Therefore, they can diffuse easily from one region to another. Gases are also highly compressible since their intermolecular distance is larger than that in solids and liquids. Thus, a **gas** is a substance that has neither a definite shape nor a definite volume.

Everyday Science

In an LPG cylinder, the gas inside the cylinder is in the liquid form under high pressure. When we turn on the knob of the cylinder, pressure is released from the liquid, which converts the liquid into the gaseous form.

▲ A gas takes the shape and volume of the tyre

Activity 4

Aim: To show that air does not have a definite shape

Materials required: Balloons of different shapes

Procedure:

1. Fill air in all the different-shaped balloons.
2. Then, deflate all the balloons.

Balloons of different shapes

Observation: Air takes the shape of the balloons it is blown into. It escapes when the balloons are deflated.

Conclusion: Air has no definite shape.

Science in Context

Both liquids and gases are called **fluids** as they are the states of matter that can flow.

Arrangement of Molecules in Gases

The intermolecular force between the molecules of gases is very weak. As a result, the gas molecules do not have contact with each other and can move around freely in any direction. Thus, the molecules in a gas are more loosely packed than in solids and liquids.

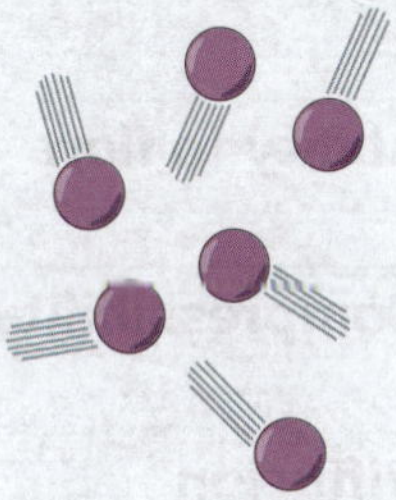

▲ Arrangement of molecules in gases

Properties of Gases

- The molecules of gases are very loosely packed.

- Gases neither have a definite shape nor a definite volume.
- Gases diffuse rapidly.
- Gases can be compressed to a high extent.

Activity 5

Aim: To demonstrate diffusion in solids, liquids and gases

Materials required: Mango juice, two glass beakers with water, stone and air freshener

Procedure:

1. Keep the beakers containing water on a table. Drop the stone in the first beaker. Observe what happens to the stone.
2. Add two spoons of mango juice in the second beaker. Note the time in which the juice completely mixes with water.
3. Spray the air freshener in one corner of the room. Note the time taken for the smell to reach your friend at the opposite corner of the room.

Observation: The stone in the water remains as it is. The mango juice mixes with water in a minute or so. Your friend gets the smell of the air freshener in a few seconds.

Conclusion: Solids cannot diffuse. Liquids can diffuse. Gases diffuse the quickest.

Table 1.1 summarizes the properties of solids, liquids and gases.

Table 1.1 Properties of solids, liquids and gases

Property	Solids	Liquids	Gases
Arrangement of molecules	Tightly packed 	Loosely packed 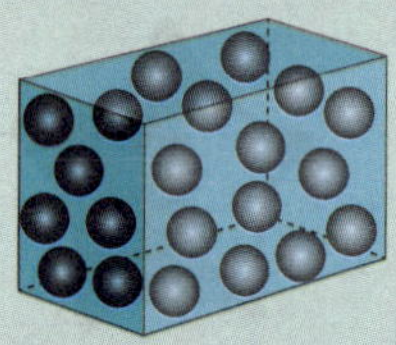	Very loosely packed 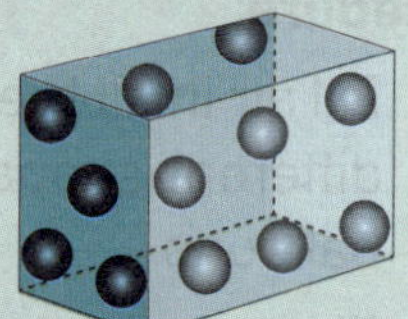
Intermolecular distance	Very small	More than in solids	More than in liquids and solids
Intermolecular force	Very strong	Weak	Very weak
Shape	Definite shape	No definite shape. It takes the shape of the container.	No definite shape. It takes the shape of the container.
Volume	Definite volume	Definite volume	No definite volume. It fills the volume of the container.
Ability to flow	Cannot flow	Flows from a higher level to a lower level	Flows in all directions
Compressibility	Incompressible	Can be compressed to some extent	Can be compressed to a great extent
Diffusion	Does not occur	Can occur easily	Can occur very easily and quickly

Keywords

Atom: the smallest particle that makes up a substance or matter

Element: a pure substance that consists of only one kind of atoms

Compound: a chemical substance formed when two or more elements combine together in a fixed ratio

In a Nutshell

- Anything that occupies space and has mass is called matter.
- Matter exists in three different states—solids, liquids and gases.
- Solids have a definite shape and volume. The molecules of a solid are closely packed.
- Liquids do not have a definite shape but have a definite volume. The molecules of a liquid are loosely packed.
- Gases neither have a definite shape nor a definite volume. The molecules of a gas are very loosely packed.

Exercise

1 Choose the correct answer for each of the following.

a. Which of the following has a definite volume but not a definite shape?

i. Chair ii. Apple

iii. Oil iv. Soap

b. Gases occupy all the available space because their molecules are

i. strong ii. weak

iii. loosely packed iv. tightly packed

c. Which of the following is the smallest particle that makes up a matter?

i. Atom ii. Molecule

iii. Compound iv. Mixture

2 Fill in the blanks.

a. Two or more atoms combine to form a __________ (compound/molecule).

b. __________ (Element/Molecule) is a pure substance that consists of only one kind of atoms.

c. __________ (Solids/Gases) neither have a definite shape nor a definite volume.

3 Write T for True and F for False.

a. Air has mass and occupies space.

b. Intermolecular space is same in all the compounds.

c. Rain water is an example of a compound.

4 Define the following terms.

a. Molecule

b. Intermolecular force

c. Liquid

5 Differentiate between the following.

a. Atom and molecule

b. Element and compound

c. Solid and gas

d. Intermolecular force and intermolecular distance

6 Give reasons for the following.

a. Solids are hard and rigid.

b. Liquids take the shape of the containers.

c. Molecules in a gas can move around freely in any direction.

7 Answer the following questions in brief.

a. What is matter? List its properties.

b. What is matter composed of?

c. What is the relationship between intermolecular distance and intermolecular force?

d. Define diffusion.

e. Write any two properties of liquids.

8 Answer the following questions in detail.

a. Explain the arrangement of molecules in solids, liquids and gases.

b. Summarize the properties of solids, liquids and gases.

c. Explain with the help of an activity that matter occupies space.

9 Think and answer.

There are 118 elements in nature but you can find more compounds than elements. Why?
(Hint: What are compounds?)

10 Project

Construct a model with the help of different colour strings and balls showing intermolecular space and force between the molecules.

11 In the Library

We have learned that an atom is the smallest unit of matter. Find out which atom has the least size and which is the largest known compound on the Earth.

Worksheet

1 Subject Integration

a. Take some ice cubes in a glass beaker and heat the beaker for a few minutes using Bunsen burner. What will happen? Depict the molecular arrangement of the states of matter that are being converted during this process in the space provided below.

b. Will the intermolecular distance remain the same during and after the heating of ice cubes? If not, why do you think so? Justify your answer.

2 Life Skills

At home, you might have noticed your mother trying to open the tightly jammed metal lids of food jars or containers by pouring hot water over the lid. What will happen by doing so? Give reasons for your answer and write it in the space given below.

Physical and Chemical Changes

2

What I shall learn

- Types of changes
- Physical changes
- Chemical changes
- Changes that involve change of energy
- Changes that involve change of state of matter

Introduction

In our everyday life, we come across various types of changes happening around us. For example, melting of ice, rotting of vegetables, dissolving of salt or sugar in water, ripening of fruits, rusting of iron, withering of leaves and flowers, changing of seasons, and growing of seedlings into plants. All these changes involve a change in the properties of the substances. As a result, substances show a change in their sizes, shapes, states, positions, colours, compositions, etc. Thus, a **change** can be defined as the conversion of any substance from one form to another.

Some changes occur on their own, while some are made to happen. Some changes are desirable while some are undesirable. Some changes happen quickly and some may take years to happen. Let us learn more about the different types of changes that occur in nature.

Types of Changes

Changes can be classified into different types which are as follows:

- Natural and artificial changes
- Reversible and irreversible changes
- Exothermic and endothermic changes
- Physical and chemical changes
- Fast and slow changes
- Periodic and non-periodic changes
- Desirable and undesirable changes

▲ Growth of a plant (natural change)

Natural and Artificial Changes

Changes that occur in nature are known as **natural changes**. Examples of natural changes are growth of a plant or a baby, ripening of a fruit, change in seasons, change of day into night, rotation and revolution of Earth, formation of fossil fuels, and occurrence of eclipses and natural disasters (like earthquake, storms and floods).

Changes that are made to happen or caused by human activities are known as **artificial changes**. Examples of artificial changes are making of a pot from clay, a dress from fibres and furniture from wood, cooking of food, construction of dams and bridges, and cutting down of trees to set up factories and cities (leading to pollution and global warming).

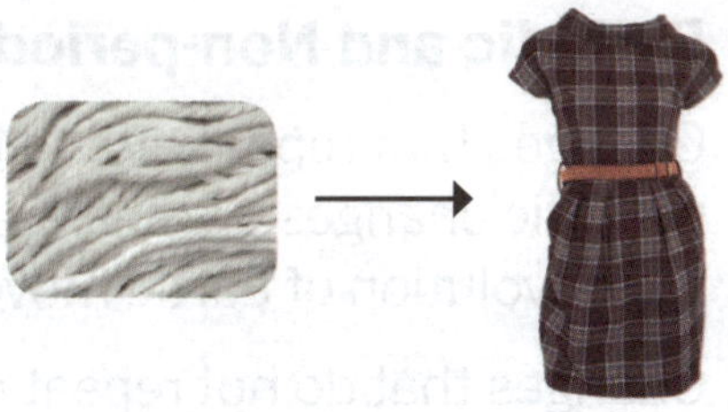

▲ Making of a dress from fibres (artificial change)

Fast and Slow Changes

Changes that take place in a very short period of time are known as **fast changes**. These changes occur spontaneously and the products are obtained almost immediately. Examples of fast changes are burning of matchsticks, paper turning into ash when burnt, occurrence of landslides, breaking of glass mirrors, bursting of firecrackers and lightning during a thunderstorm.

▲ Burning of paper (fast change)

Greenathon

Collect the seeds of the fruits you eat. Wash the seeds and store them. Whenever you go on a trip, plant these seeds in any barren land that you see. This will help in the growth of new trees.

Changes that take place over a long period of time are known as **slow changes**. These changes may take hours, days, weeks, months or years to occur. Examples of slow changes are growth of a baby into an adult, formation of fossil fuels, germination of seeds, rusting of iron, growth of fingernails and decay of dead plants.

▲ Germination of seeds (slow change)

Reversible and Irreversible Changes

Changes that can be reversed, that is, we can get back the original substance by changing the conditions that brought about the change, are known as **reversible changes**. In such changes, there might be a change in the look and feel of the substance, but no new substance is formed during or after the change. Thus, the properties of the substance do not change and the change is temporary. Examples of reversible changes are melting of ice, stretching of a rubber band, folding and unfolding of paper, blowing of air into a balloon, boiling of water and dissolving of salt or sugar in water.

▲ Melting of ice (reversible change)

Changes that cannot be reversed, that is, we cannot get back the original substance by changing the conditions that brought about the change, are known as **irreversible changes**. Such changes form new substances during or after the change. Thus, the properties of the substance change and the change is permanent. Examples of irreversible changes are growth of living things, cooking of rice, ripening of fruits, burning of wood, digestion of food and withering of leaves.

▲ Growth of a baby into an adult (irreversible change)

Periodic and Non-periodic Changes

Changes that repeat after a fixed interval of time are known as **periodic changes**. Examples of periodic changes are change in seasons, phases of the moon, cycle of day and night, rotation and revolution of Earth, movements of the hands of a clock and our heartbeat.

Changes that do not repeat after a fixed interval of time and can occur any time are known as **non-periodic changes**. Examples of non-periodic changes are occurrence of cyclones, earthquakes, tsunamis, volcanic eruptions, accidents and rain showers, and sneezing.

Do You Know?

Comets are also differentiated into periodic and non-periodic based on their occurrences.

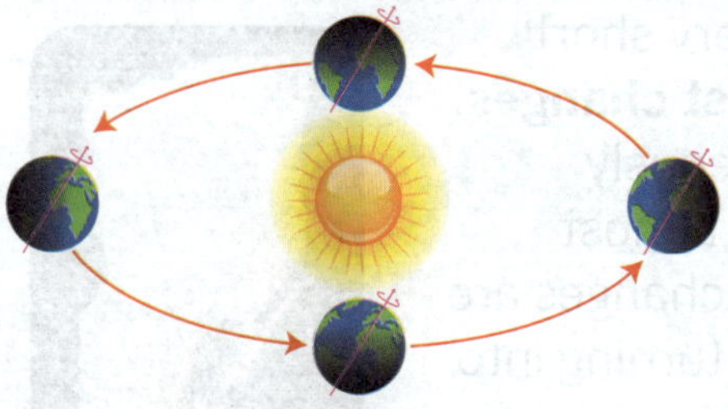

▲ Revolution of Earth (periodic change)

▲ Volcanic eruption (non-periodic change)

Exothermic and Endothermic Changes

Changes in which there is release of energy in the form of heat are known as **exothermic changes**. Examples of exothermic changes are burning of fuels, bursting of crackers, condensation of water vapour and freezing of water to form ice cubes.

Changes in which there is absorption of energy in the form of heat are known as **endothermic changes**. Examples of endothermic changes are photosynthesis in green plants, cooking of food, evaporation of water and melting of ice cubes.

Do You Know?

When you apply nail polish remover, you feel a cooling effect on your fingers and toes. This is because the acetone present in the nail polish remover absorbs heat from your body while evaporating.

▲ Bursting of crackers (exothermic change)

▲ Photosynthesis (endothermic change)

▲ Cooking of food (desirable change)

Desirable and Undesirable Changes

Changes that are useful to us are known as **desirable changes**. Examples of desirable changes are fermentation of grape juice into wine, formation of curd from milk, cooking of food, ripening of fruits and blooming of flowers.

Changes that are harmful to us are known as **undesirable changes**. Examples of undesirable changes are spoilage of food, occurrence of earthquakes, storms and floods, rotting of fruits and vegetables, soil erosion and rusting of iron.

A change can be desirable at one time or undesirable at another time based on the situation in which it occurs. A few examples are given below:

- Rain is desirable as it fills up seas, rivers and lakes, but if the same rain occurs in excess and causes floods, it results in loss of both property and life.
- Cutting down of trees for industrialization is desirable as it provides employment to many people, but at the same time, forests are lost which leads to rise in carbon dioxide levels and thus global warming.
- Burning of fossil fuels releases energy that is used in many ways. But along with energy, poisonous gases like carbon monoxide and sulphur dioxide are released that lead to air pollution, which is undesirable.

▲Flood (undesirable change)

Find Out

Classify the following into desirable and undesirable changes: formation of curd, tsunami, growth of a plant and breaking of a glass vase.

Revision Zone

Write T for True and F for False.

1. Germination of seeds is an example of a slow change.
2. Cutting of trees is an artificial change.
3. Cyclones occur periodically.
4. Withering of leaves is an irreversible change.

Physical and Chemical Changes

Let us look in detail at physical and chemical changes.

Physical Changes

Changes in which no new substances are formed are known as **physical changes**. Such changes might alter the physical properties of the original substance, but the chemical properties remain the same. For example, melting of butter, tearing or folding of paper, cutting of an iron rod into pieces, and boiling, evaporation and condensation of a substance.

(a) Melting of butter

(b) Tearing of paper

▲ Physical changes

Characteristics of Physical Changes

- No new products are formed.
- There might be a change in the physical properties of the substance, such as shape, size, state, colour and density.

Science in Context

Recycling of plastic or iron is a reversible process. It is a physical change as the properties of iron or plastic do not change.

- Chemical properties and composition of the original substance do not change at all.
- Physical changes are mostly temporary and can be reversible or irreversible in nature. For example, melting of ice is a reversible change, whereas breaking of glass is an irreversible change.
- The change in energy is less during physical changes.

Examples of Physical Changes

Melting of ice We know that when ice is heated, it melts to form water. In this process, no new substance is formed. The chemical properties of water remain the same whether it is in the solid state (ice) or the liquid state (water) as both are made up of water molecules. Only the shape and the state of matter change in both this process. This change is temporary and reversible. Hence, melting of ice is a physical change.

▲ Wet clothes dry faster on a sunny day

Evaporation The process in which a liquid gets converted into its vapour state is known as **evaporation**. The water molecules in the vapour state have the same chemical properties as those in the liquid state. Only the physical state of the liquid changes. Also, no new substances are formed. Hence, evaporation is a physical change.

Drying of clothes We have seen that wet clothes dry quickly on a sunny day due to evaporation. This is because the process of evaporation increases as the temperature of the surroundings increases. Thus, drying of clothes is also a physical change.

Activity 1

Aim: To prove that evaporation is a physical change

Materials required: Two beakers, Bunsen burner, water, tripod stand, wire gauze, matchbox, laboratory stand and a lid

Procedure:

1. Take a beaker containing water.
2. Place the beaker on the Bunsen burner and start heating the water.
3. Set up the apparatus as in the figure given alongside.

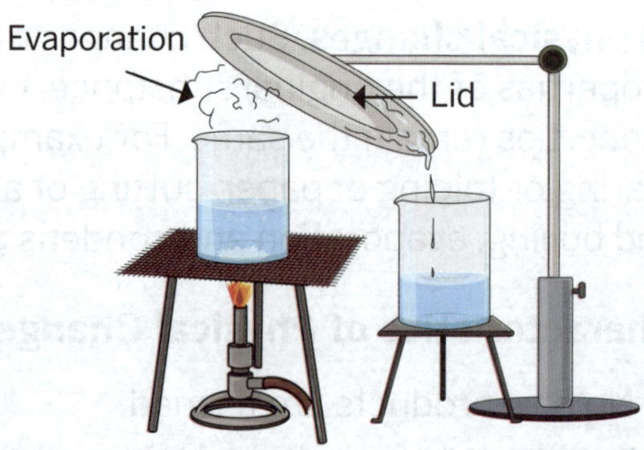

Observation: Upon heating, the water gradually converts into water vapour. When the vapour comes in contact with the cool surface of the lid, it condenses and converts back into liquid water.

Conclusion: Evaporation is a physical change as no new product is formed.

Dissolving The process in which a solid is mixed or dissolved in a liquid to form a solution is known as **dissolution**. When salt is dissolved in a liquid, it forms a mixture. Through evaporation and condensation processes, we can separate the salt (solute) and the liquid (solvent). The salt and the liquid, thus, obtained do not undergo any change in their chemical properties. Also, no new substances are formed. Hence, dissolution is a physical change.

Chemical Changes

Changes in which new substances are formed are known as **chemical changes**. Such changes alter both physical and chemical properties of the original substances. For example, burning of paper, rotting of fruits and vegetables, cooking of food and baking of a cake.

Characteristics of Chemical Changes

- New products are formed.
- Chemical composition and properties of the original substance change.
- Chemical changes are irreversible and permanent in nature.
- Energy change is more during chemical changes than during physical changes.
- During a chemical change, energy is produced in the form of heat or light.

▲ Burning of wood

Examples of Chemical Changes

Burning of any substance (like fuels and firecrackers) When a piece of wood or a cracker is burned, it combines with the oxygen in the air to form products like smoke, ashes, carbon dioxide and water vapour. Also, heat and light are released during this change. The properties of the new products formed are different from those of the original substances. We cannot get back wood or cracker from the ashes. So, it is a permanent and an irreversible change. Hence, burning of any substance is a chemical change.

▲ Rusted object

Rusting of iron The process in which iron objects form a reddish-brown, flaky substance on their surface when they come in contact with moisture and oxygen present in the air is known as **rusting**. The reddish-brown deposit formed on the iron objects is known as **rust**. It is a chemical change as the iron cannot be obtained back from the rust.

Everyday Science

Rusting results in the loss of iron objects. Hence, to prevent rusting, ensure that the iron objects do not come in contact with moisture and oxygen. This can be done by painting, electroplating or applying grease or oil on their surface.

Curdling of milk Curdling is a process that involves conversion of milk into curd by a bacterium called **lactobacillus**. This bacterium converts lactose (a kind of sugar) present in the milk to lactic acid. This gives the sour taste to the curd. The properties of curd are different from those of milk. It is an irreversible change as we cannot get back milk from the curd. Hence, it is a chemical change.

▲ Curdling of milk

▲ Cooked food

Cooking of food While cooking food, heat energy is needed which results in the formation of new substances. Properties of the new substances are different from those of the original raw ingredients used for cooking and we cannot get back the raw ingredients. Hence, it is a chemical change.

Reaction of iron powder with sulphur powder When iron powder (iron filings) and sulphur powder are mixed and heated, they form ferrous sulphide (FeS). The new substance formed has properties different from iron (Fe) and sulphur (S). Therefore, heating a mixture of iron and sulphur powder is a chemical change.

Differences between physical and chemical changes are listed in Table 2.1.

Table 2.1 Differences between physical and chemical changes

Physical change	Chemical change
Physical properties of substances might change. Chemical properties do not change at all.	Both chemical and physical properties of substances are changed.
Most of the changes are temporary and reversible.	All the changes are permanent and irreversible.
No new products are formed.	New products are formed with properties different from the original substance(s).
Negligible amount of energy is absorbed or released.	A significant amount of energy is absorbed or released.

Challenge Yourself

You might have noticed that cut pieces of some vegetables and fruits like potato, apple, etc., turn brown when exposed to air if they are not consumed immediately. Do you know what kind of a change it is?

Revision Zone

Categorize the following changes into physical and chemical changes.

Burning of paper, rusting, melting of ice, evaporation, cooking of food

Physical changes: ____________________

Chemical changes: ____________________

Challenge Yourself

Think of a few examples from daily life which involve both physical and chemical changes.

Changes That Involve Change of Energy

When a change occurs, there is either absorption or release of energy. The energy released or absorbed can be in the form of heat, light, sound, etc. The amount of energy absorbed or released may differ depending upon the type of change occurring.

Energy Changes in a Physical Change

In physical changes, the energy change is minimal and even negligible in a few cases. One of the most distinct changes that occurs during a physical change is the change of state. Energy is required or given out to either increase or decrease the intermolecular force of attraction between molecules of the substance undergoing change. For example, ice absorbs heat energy upon melting, whereas water releases heat energy upon freezing. In order to boil or evaporate water, energy is used in the form of heat.

Energy Changes in a Chemical Change

In chemical changes, the amount of energy change is more than that in physical changes as the properties of the original substances change completely to form new products. For example, during burning of fuels, a large amount of energy is released and this energy is used to cook food and run automobiles. Plants use sunlight (energy) to prepare their food by the process of photosynthesis.

Table 2.2 gives a few examples of changes and their energy changes.

Table 2.2 List of some changes and their energy changes

Change	Energy change
Burning of wood (chemical change)	Heat energy is released
Bursting of crackers (chemical change)	Heat energy is released
Melting of ice (physical change)	Heat energy is absorbed
Photosynthesis (chemical change)	Heat energy is absorbed
Boiling of water (physical change)	Heat energy is absorbed

Changes That Involve Change of State of Matter

Most of the physical changes involve change of state of matter. Let us discuss some examples in which the change of state of matter happen.

Melting and freezing The process in which a solid gets converted into its liquid state when heated is known as **melting**. The process in which a liquid gets converted into its solid state when cooled is known as **freezing**. For example, when ice is heated, it melts to form water and when this water is cooled, it freezes and turns back into ice. Here, no new substance is formed. The chemical properties of water remain the same whether it is in the solid state (ice) or the liquid state (water). Only the shape and the state of matter change in both the processes. These changes are temporary and reversible.

Boiling When water is heated, it starts boiling and then changes into vapour. The process in which a liquid gets converted into its vapour state when heated at a particular temperature is known as **boiling**. The chemical properties of water molecules remain the same in both liquid and vapour states. No new substances are formed during boiling.

Evaporation and condensation The process in which a liquid gets converted into its vapour state is known as **evaporation**. The process of evaporation takes place at a temperature

> **Science in Context**
> Solid air fresheners are sublimable substances. They sublime and release vapour giving out a pleasant aroma.

below the boiling point of the liquid. When the vapour is cooled, it gets converted back into its liquid state. This process is called **condensation**. The vapour formed does not have any new chemical properties except the change in its physical state. Also, no new substances are formed during these processes.

Sublimation The process in which a solid gets converted into its vapour state directly without passing through its liquid state is known as **sublimation**. When the vapour is condensed, it converts back into its solid state. There are no new products formed. Camphor, naphthalene balls, ammonium chloride and iodine salts are examples of substances that sublime. Hence, sublimation is an example of a physical change.

Activity 2

Aim: To demonstrate that sublimation is a physical change

Materials required: China dish, ammonium chloride crystals, Bunsen burner, a glass funnel, tripod stand, cotton and spatula

Procedure:

1. Take a clean China dish and place half a spatula of ammonium chloride crystals in it.
2. Place the China dish over the tripod stand.
3. Cover the China dish with an inverted glass funnel. Seal the narrow end of the funnel with the help of a cotton plug.
4. Start heating the ammonium chloride crystals using a Bunsen burner.
5. Allow the set-up to cool down. Observe carefully and record the observations before heating, after heating and after cooling.

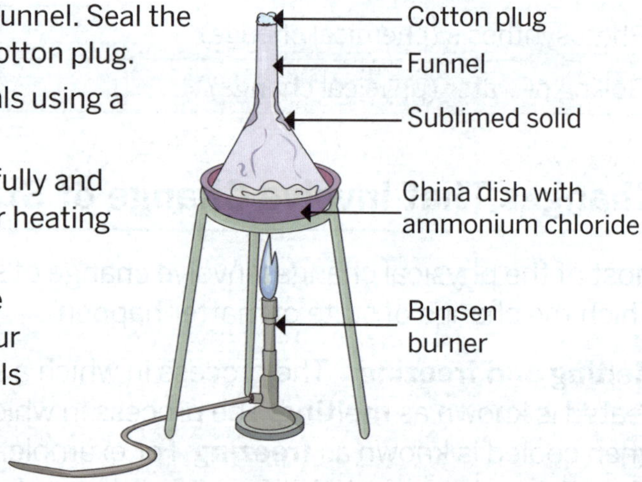

Observation: On heating, the ammonium chloride crystals change to vapour. When cooled, the vapour changes back to solid form and deposits as crystals along the inner walls of the funnel.

Conclusion: Sublimation is a physical change as no new product is formed.

Revision Zone

Fill in the blanks with the correct words.

1. In physical changes, the energy change is __________ (maximum/minimal).
2. The process in which a solid gets converted into its liquid state when heated is known as __________ (melting/freezing).
3. The process of evaporation takes place at a temperature below the __________ (melting/boiling) point of the liquid.

Keywords

Change: the conversion of any substance from one form to another

Periodic changes: changes that repeat after a fixed time interval

Non-periodic changes: changes that occur any time and do not repeat after a fixed time interval

Exothermic changes: changes in which there is release of heat energy

Endothermic changes: changes in which there is absorption of heat energy

Physical changes: changes in which no new substances are formed

Dissolution: the process of solids dissolving in liquids to form a solution

Chemical changes: changes in which new substances are formed, and physical and chemical properties are altered

In a Nutshell

- Changes are classified into different types: natural and artificial, fast and slow, reversible and irreversible, periodic and non-periodic, desirable and undesirable, exothermic and endothermic, and physical and chemical.
- Physical changes alter the physical properties (shape, size, colour, state or density) of the original substance.
- Chemical changes alter the physical as well as the chemical properties of the original substance.
- During most physical changes, there is change of state of matter that is reversible.
- During a change, there is either absorption or release of energy in the form of heat, light or sound.

Exercise

1 Choose the correct answer for each of the following.

a. Which of the following is not an irreversible change?

i. Melting of wax

ii. Boiling of vegetables

iii. Baking of biscuits

iv. Frying of food products

b. Which of the following is a periodic change?

i. Cyclone   ii. Phases of moon

iii. Accident   iv. Tsunami

c. Burning of petrol is an example of __________ change.

i. physical   ii. endothermic

iii. exothermic   iv. None of these

d. Digestion of food is an example of __________ change.

i. physical   ii. reversible

iii. chemical   iv. undesirable

e. Which of these is a physical change?

i. Rusting of iron

ii. Burning of paper

iii. Folding of paper

iv. Cooking of food

f. Identify the characteristic of a chemical change.

i. Change in both physical and chemical properties

ii. No new products are formed

iii. Temporary and reversible

iv. Energy change is minimal

2 Fill in the blanks.

a. Cutting down of trees is a/an __________ (natural/artificial) change.

b. Germination of seeds is a __________ (fast/slow) change.

c. The products of a/an __________ (desirable/undesirable) change are harmful and unpleasing.

d. The changes in which there is release of heat energy are called __________ (exothermic/endothermic) changes.

e. If the chemical properties of a substance remain unchanged but its shape changes, it is a __________ (chemical/physical) change.

f. The new products formed in a chemical change show __________ (same/new) properties.

3 Write T for True and F for False.

a. Burning of a matchstick is a fast change.

b. All changes in nature are reversible.

c. Occurrence of landslides is a periodic change.

d. In a physical change, the chemical properties of a substance change.

e. Sublimation is an example of a physical change.

f. Rotting of vegetables is an example of a chemical change.

4 Give an example for each of the following.

a. Natural change

b. Fast change

c. Non-periodic change

d. Undesirable change

e. Reversible change

5 Define the following terms.

a. Desirable changes

b. Exothermic changes

c. Boiling

d. Dissolution

e. Rusting

6 Differentiate between the following.

a. Natural and artificial changes

b. Fast and slow changes

c. Periodic and non-periodic changes

d. Melting and freezing

e. Boiling and evaporation

7 Give reasons for the following.

a. Bursting of crackers is an exothermic change.

b. Boiling is a physical change.

c. All chemical changes are permanent.

d. Rusting of iron is a chemical change.

8 Answer the following questions in brief.

a. Distinguish between desirable and undesirable changes.

b. Define endothermic change.

c. Give two examples of physical change which are irreversible.

d. How are the following changes different from each other?

  i. Changing of milk into curd

  ii. Hot milk becoming cold milk

e. Give two examples each of physical and chemical changes.

f. Is magnetization of an iron nail a physical change? Explain.

9 Answer the following questions in detail.

a. Distinguish between reversible and irreversible changes. Explain with the help of examples.

b. A change can be desirable at one time or undesirable at another time. Justify this statement with examples.

c. What are the differences between physical and chemical changes?

d. Explain evaporation as a physical change.

e. Explain the following.

  i. Rusting of iron

  ii. Curdling of milk

f. Explain the concept of energy changes in physical and chemical changes with examples.

10 Think and answer.

a. Seema says that rusting of an iron screw is an irreversible change, while Reema says that it is an irreversible change. Who do you think is correct and why?

b. The burning of a candle is a physical as well as a chemical change. Justify your answer.

11 Project

Take a few green grams. Soak them in water overnight. Remove the green grams from water and tie them in a wet cotton cloth. Keep the cloth moist by sprinkling water from time to time. Observe the green gram after one day. You can see the formation of sprouts. Observe and record the changes in the sprouts for a week. Record your observations in the form of a chart and specify what kind of a change it is.

12 In the Library

Find out what kind of a change is the process of digestion of food that takes place in our body. Prepare a report on your findings.

Worksheet

1 Subject Integration

Some of the changes involve the absorption or release of energy in the form of heat. While playing outdoors on a hot sunny day, we sweat a lot. Is sweating an exothermic or endothermic change? Give reasons for your answer.

____

____

____

2 Life Skills

Melting of ice is a physical change and the process of photosynthesis is a chemical change. But both these natural processes share one common thing in terms of energy change. What is that?

Melting of ice

Photosynthesis

____

____

____

Elements, Compounds and Mixtures (Experimental Techniques)

3

What I shall learn

- Elements
- Compounds
- Representation of elements and compounds using symbols and formulae
- Types of mixtures
- Separation techniques

Introduction

We use a variety of substances in our daily life. Each substance around us is made of matter. For example, the food we eat, the water we drink, the air we breathe, non-living objects like table, book, stars and clouds, and living things are all made of matter. We studied in class 6 that each substance has a unique composition. Based on their composition, all substances (or matter) in nature can be broadly classified into pure and mixed substances. Mixed substances are also called mixtures or impure substances. Most of the substances found in nature are mixtures. Can you recall the characteristics of pure substances and mixtures learned in class 6?

Pure Substances

A substance that consists of only one kind of atoms or molecules is called a **pure substance**. In pure substances, atoms or molecules combine in a fixed proportion, that is, they have a fixed chemical composition. Pure substances exhibit their own distinct set of properties. They can be classified into two types: elements and compounds. Elements like oxygen and copper, and compounds like water and carbon dioxide are a few examples of pure substances.

Elements

A substance that consists of only one kind of atoms is called an **element**. The smallest unit of an element is an atom. For example, the element gold contains only one kind of atoms, that is, gold atoms. Other examples of elements are carbon, sodium and oxygen. We know that all the atoms that make up an element are of the same kind, but two different elements cannot have the same kind of atoms. For instance, atoms of oxygen and atoms of hydrogen are different from each other. So, every element has its own unique properties.

▲ Gold (element)

So far, nearly 118 elements have been discovered. Of these, 98 elements are found naturally on Earth and the remaining

Remember

On the basis of their properties, elements can be classified into two broad classes: metals and non-metals.

Metals are generally solid at room temperature. They are hard, lustrous, malleable, ductile and sonorous in nature. Examples: iron, copper, silver and zinc.

Non-metals are solid or gaseous at room temperature. They are brittle, non-lustrous, non-malleable, non-ductile and non-sonorous in nature. Examples: carbon, oxygen hydrogen and sulphur.

Certain elements exhibit the properties of both metals and non-metals. They are called **metalloids**. Examples: silicon, boron and germanium.

20 elements have been prepared artificially by scientists in laboratories.

Characteristics of Elements

- Elements are pure substances that consist of only one kind of atoms.
- Each element has its own unique properties.
- The atoms of an element exhibit the same properties as the element.
- Elements cannot be separated or broken down into simpler components by physical or chemical methods.

How to Represent Elements

Elements or atoms of an element are represented using symbols. The representation of an element using the short form or abbreviation of its name is known as its **chemical symbol**.

In earlier times, the elements were represented pictorially. Later, the elements were named after the name of the place where they were first found. For example, the name copper and its symbol Cu come from the Latin word *cuprum*, which means 'from the island of Cyprus'. In the modern method of representing elements, letters representing the names of the elements are used as symbols.

Features of the modern method of representation are as follows.

- The first letter of the name of the element is used as the symbol. The first letter is written as a capital letter. For example, H for hydrogen, O for oxygen and C for carbon. The English names of these elements are similar to their Latin names.
- If two or more elements have their English names starting with the same alphabet, then a two-letter symbol is used. The first letter of the name is the first letter of the symbol and the next non-repeating letter of the name is the second letter of the symbol. The first letter is written as a capital letter and the second letter is written as a small letter. For example, Ca for calcium, Cd for cadmium, Cl for chlorine and Co for cobalt.
- In some cases, the English names and the Latin names of the elements are different. So, for these elements, the symbols are derived from their Latin names. For example, the Latin name of potassium is *kalium* and its symbol is K. Similarly, the Latin name of gold is *aurum* and its symbol is Au.

Do You Know?

Some elements that exist in free state or in uncombined form in nature are gold, platinum, silver and copper. These are called **native elements**.

Table 3.1 Some elements and their symbols

Element	Symbol	Element	Symbol
Helium	He	Phosphorus	P
Nitrogen	N	Magnesium	Mg
Iodine	I	Manganese	Mn
Aluminium	Al	Argon	Ar
Zinc	Zn	Platinum	Pt

Table 3.2 Some elements with their Latin names and symbols

Element	Latin name	Symbol
Sodium	*Natrium*	Na
Iron	*Ferrum*	Fe
Copper	*Cuprum*	Cu
Silver	*Argentum*	Ag
Mercury	*Hydrargyrum*	Hg

Know the Scientist

John Dalton (1766–1844) was the first scientist to use symbols to represent elements. He was an English chemist, who postulated the atomic theory. He was the first person to explain the difference between an atom and a molecule. His theory supports the law of conservation of mass.

Compounds

The chemical substance formed when two or more atoms of different elements combine chemically in a fixed proportion is called a **compound**. A compound is made up of molecules of same kind. For example, water contains only one kind of molecules, that is, water molecules. Other examples of compounds are carbon dioxide, salt and sugar.

Characteristics of Compounds

- Compounds are pure substances formed when two or more atoms of different elements combine together chemically in a fixed proportion.
- The properties of compounds are different from the properties of their constituent elements.
- Compounds exhibit their own physical and chemical properties.
- Compounds can be separated into their individual components by chemical methods.

Formation of Compounds

Compounds are formed when a chemical bond is created between atoms either by the transfer of electrons from one atom to another atom or by the sharing of electrons between two atoms of different elements or two atoms of the same element. Here, we will learn how compounds are formed by the transfer of electrons between atoms.

Know the Scientist

J J Berzelius (1779–1848) was a Swedish chemist who made several contributions to the field of chemistry. He was the first person to suggest that the first one or two letters of the names of elements can be used as symbols. He identified the elements thorium, silicon, cerium and selenium.
He is popularly known as the father of Swedish chemistry.

When two or more atoms of different elements combine together, one of the atoms loses one or more of its electrons and these electrons are gained by the other atom. This results in the formation of respective ions, that is, a cation and an anion. As these ions carry opposite charges, they are attracted towards each other. Due to this force of attraction between the oppositely charged ions, a chemical bond is formed. This chemical bond holds the combining ions together leading to the formation of a compound.

How to Represent Compounds

Just as we represent elements by their chemical symbols, compounds can be represented by chemical formulae. A chemical formula is the representation of a compound using the symbols of its constituent elements. In other words, the symbolic representation of the composition of a chemical compound is known as its **chemical formula**. It exhibits the different elements present in a molecule of a compound and the number of atoms of each combining or constituent element it contains. For example, the chemical formula of carbon dioxide is CO_2. This indicates that a molecule of CO_2 consists of one atom of carbon and two atoms of oxygen.

We can easily write the chemical formula of a compound if we know the symbols and valencies of atoms of the different elements forming the compound. Follow the steps given below to write the chemical formula of a compound.

1. Write the symbols of the elements or radicals/ions that form the compound.
2. The metallic part (positive ion) of the compound should always be written first followed by the non-metallic part (negative ion).
3. Write their valencies on top of their symbols as superscripts.
4. If the valencies are identical, cancel the valencies. If the valencies are different, then interchange the valencies with respect to the symbols by making arrows and write them as subscripts.
5. Simplify the formula by dividing the valencies by a common factor, if divisible.
6. If the compound contains compound radicals, then the radicals are enclosed in brackets and the number is written outside the brackets as subscript. For instance, the valency of magnesium (Mg^{2+}) is two and that of nitrate (NO_3^-) is one. Thus, the chemical formula of magnesium nitrate is written as $Mg(NO_3)_2$.
7. The valencies 1 need not be written in the final formula.

Find Out

Why is it important to know the valencies to write a chemical formula?

Keeping in mind the above steps, let us write the chemical formulae of some compounds.

Writing the Formulae of Chlorides

Calcium chloride

Step 1: Ca Cl (Write the symbols of the constituent elements, here calcium and chlorine)

Step 2: Ca^2 Cl^1 (Write the valency of each element as superscript)

Step 3: Ca^2 Cl^1 (Interchange the valencies and write them as subscripts)
Ca_1 Cl_2

Step 4: Ca_1 Cl_2 (Divide the valencies by a common factor, if divisible)

Chemical formula of calcium chloride: $CaCl_2$ (Valency 1 need not be written)

Writing the Formulae of Oxides

Magnesium oxide

Step 1: Mg O

Step 2: Mg^2 O^2

Step 3: Mg^2 O^2

Mg_2 O_2

Step 4: Mg_2 O_2 (Divide the valencies by a common factor, here 2)

Mg_1 O_1

Chemical formula of magnesium oxide: MgO

Writing the Formulae of Sulphides

Sodium sulphide

Step 1: Na S

Step 2: Na^1 S^2

Step 3: Na^1 S^2

Na_2 S_1

Step 4: Na_2 S_1

Chemical formula of sodium sulphide: Na_2S

Significance of a Chemical Formula

The following information can be drawn from a chemical formula:

- The chemical name of the compound
- The elements present in the compound
- The number of atoms of each element present in one molecule of the compound
- The chemical formula represents one molecule of the compound

Remember

In a chemical formula, the subscript denotes the number of atoms of the element present in one molecule of the compound. For example, in Fe_2S_3, there are 2 atoms of iron and 3 atoms of sulphur.

Table 3.3 Few compounds with their constituent elements and formulae

Compound	Constituent elements	Formula	Compound	Constituent elements	Formula
Methane	Carbon (C) Hydrogen(H)	CH_4	Sulphur dioxide	Sulphur (S) Oxygen (O)	SO_2
Sodium hydroxide	Sodium (Na) Oxygen (O) Hydrogen (H)	NaOH	Sulphuric acid	Hydrogen (H) Sulphur (S) Oxygen (O)	H_2SO_4
Calcium hydroxide	Calcium (Ca) Oxygen (O) Hydrogen (H)	$Ca(OH)_2$	Copper sulphate	Copper (Cu) Sulphur (S) Oxygen (O)	$CuSO_4$
Potassium nitrate	Potassium (K) Nitrogen (N) Oxygen (O)	KNO_3	Calcium carbonate	Calcium (Ca) Carbon (C) Oxygen (O)	$CaCO_3$

Revision Zone

Match the compounds with their chemical formulae.

1. Copper (II) chloride	a. CaS
2. Zinc oxide	b. $CuCl_2$
3. Sodium oxide	c. ZnO
4. Calcium sulphide	d. Na_2O

Mixture

A **mixture** is a substance that contains two or more different substances (elements, compounds or both) mixed together in such a way that no chemical change occurs between them. The different types of substances present in a mixture are called its **components** or **constituents**. Air, tap water, oil in water, sugar in water, soil and alloys are a few examples of mixtures.

Characteristics of Mixtures

- A mixture does not exhibit any characteristic property of its own. The components of a mixture do not lose their properties and thus retain their original properties in the mixture.
- In a mixture, the components are not present in any fixed ratio or proportion.
- The components of a mixture can be separated easily through physical methods of separation.
- Mixtures are not pure substances as they contain more than one type of component.

▲ Mixture of pulses

Table 3.4 gives the comparison between compounds and mixtures.

Table 3.4 Comparison between compounds and mixtures

Compounds	Mixtures
A compound is made up of two or more elements mixed together chemically.	A mixture is made up of two or more substances that are not mixed together chemically.
Compounds exhibit new properties. They do not show the properties of their constituent elements.	Mixtures do not exhibit new properties. They retain the same properties of their individual components.
The ratio of components in a compound is fixed.	The ratio of components in a mixture is not fixed.
The components of a compound cannot be separated by physical methods.	The components of a mixture can be separated by physical methods.
Compounds are pure substances.	Mixtures are impure substances.

Types of Mixtures

1. Based on the distribution of components, mixtures can be classified as homogeneous and heterogeneous mixtures.

Homogeneous Mixtures

When the components in a mixture are distributed uniformly and cannot be seen distinctly, it is called a **homogeneous mixture**. The properties of a homogeneous mixture remain the same in all parts of the mixture. Air is a homogeneous mixture.

Solutions and alloys are examples of homogeneous mixtures. In a **solution**, the solute particles (salt or sugar) dissolve in a solvent (water) completely. Thus, the individual components in a homogeneous mixture cannot be seen distinctly. Examples of solutions are salt solution, sugar solution, sea water, honey and orange juice.

An **alloy** is a mixture of two or more metals, or metals and non-metals. Examples of alloys are stainless steel, bronze and brass.

▲ Honey (homogeneous mixture)

Heterogeneous Mixtures

When the components that make up a mixture are not distributed uniformly and can be seen distinctly, it is called a **heterogeneous mixture**. The properties of a heterogeneous mixture differ in different parts of the mixture. Smoke is a heterogeneous mixture.

Suspensions and emulsions are examples of heterogeneous mixtures. A **suspension** contains small, undissolved solid particles suspended in a fluid (a liquid or a gas). These particles can be seen distinctly. When the suspension is kept undisturbed, the particles settle down. A few examples of suspensions are chalk powder in water, dust in air and muddy water.

An **emulsion** is a mixture of two or more immiscible liquids (liquids that do not mix together completely and form separate layers when mixed). An emulsion of oil and water is an example of a heterogeneous mixture in which oil and water are seen as two separate layers.

▲ Oil in water (heterogeneous mixture)

2. Based on the state of the components, mixtures can be classified into three types.

Mixtures

- Solid–solid mixture
  Examples: salt and pepper, husk in rice and soil
- Solid–liquid mixture
  Examples: sugar solution, sand and water, and copper sulphate solution
- Liquid–liquid mixture
  Examples: water and milk, oil and water, and alcohol and water

Separation of Mixtures

We know that a mixture is not a pure substance. It consists of different types of components. Of these components, some may be useful and some may not be of use. To use only the desirable components, separation is required. Separation of mixtures is necessary due to the following reasons:

- To separate useful components from a mixture. For example, by churning milk, cream is separated from milk so that both the components can be used appropriately.
- To remove unwanted materials or impurities from a mixture. For example, separation of husk from rice grains, unwanted stones from rice grains or pulses before cooking and separation of unwanted leaves from raw leafy vegetables.
- To get desirable or pure substances. For example, in preparation of tea, tea leaves are separated from brewed tea.

Methods of Separating Mixtures

Different components of a mixture have different chemical and physical properties. Hence, selecting the appropriate method of separation for a mixture depends on the characteristic properties of each component.

Some separation techniques of mixtures into their components are discussed in the following sections.

Separating Solid–Solid Mixtures

Sublimation

The process in which a solid changes directly into its gaseous state without passing through its liquid state is called sublimation.

Principle: This method is used when a mixture contains a component that can sublime.

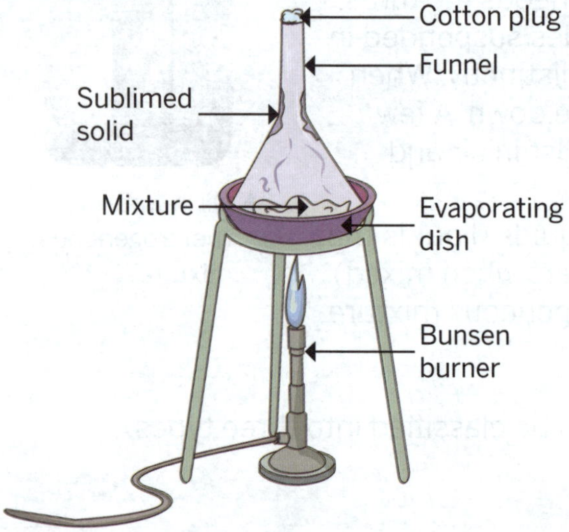

▲ Sublimation

The set-up for sublimation is shown below. In this method, the mixture is taken in an evaporating dish. When the mixture is heated, the solid component that sublimes evaporates as vapours, leaving behind the component that does not sublime in the dish. Then, the sublimed solid is obtained by cooling the vapours. Thus, the mixture is separated.

Iodine, camphor and ammonium chloride are sublimable substances.

Separating Solid–Liquid Mixtures

To separate solid–liquid mixtures, the selection of the appropriate method depends on whether the solid component is soluble or insoluble in the liquid.

The following methods are used for separating a solid–liquid mixture when the solid is soluble in the liquid.

Evaporation

The process in which a liquid changes into its gaseous state is called **evaporation**.

Principle: This method involves the evaporation of the liquid component from the mixture while the solid component is left behind. In this method, the liquid component is allowed to evaporate either by heating or by exposing the mixture to sunlight. The evaporated liquid escapes into the atmosphere and thus leaves behind only the solid component.

Evaporation is used to obtain common salt from sea water. Sea water contains large amounts of salt dissolved in it. It is allowed to flow through narrow channels near coastal areas and is then collected in shallow ponds (called **salt pans**). The water in these salt pans is allowed to dry in the sun. As the water evaporates, solid crystals of salt are left behind. The salt is then collected and sent for purification. The purified salt is used for various purposes.

Activity 1

Aim: To demonstrate the separation of salt from salt solution using evaporation method

Materials required: China dish, salt solution, wire gauze, Bunsen burner and tripod stand

Procedure:

1. Take some salt solution in a China dish.
2. Heat the solution using a Bunsen burner.
3. Boil the solution until the liquid evaporates completely.

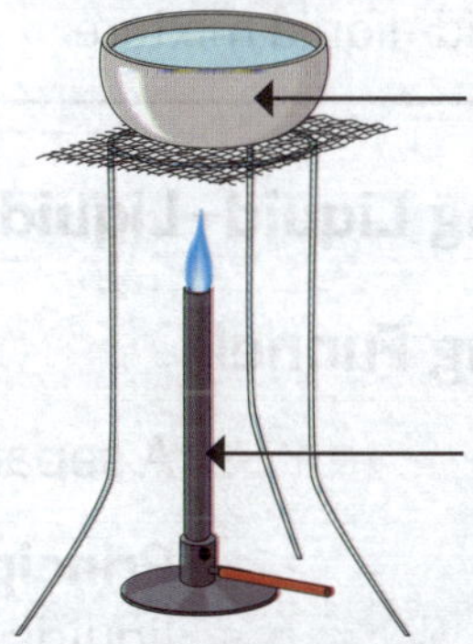

Observation: The solid, white particles of salt are left behind along the inner sides of the China dish after evaporation.

Conclusion: Soluble solids present in a solid–liquid mixture can be separated by evaporation method.

Distillation

A separation method used to separate a pure liquid from a mixture or solution by evaporation and then condensation is called **distillation**. The process of distillation is carried out in a special laboratory apparatus. The process involves the following steps:

1. The mixture is heated in a round-bottomed flask. Due to heating, the liquid component in the mixture evaporates to form vapours and the solid component is left behind in the flask.
2. A condenser is fitted to the flask. The vapours of the liquid rise and pass through this condenser where they cool down and condense to form pure liquid.
3. This pure liquid is collected in a separate flask.

This method is used to obtain distilled water, which is the purest form of water, as it does not contain any impurities. It is used in science laboratories, car batteries and medicines.

Do You Know?

In Kuwait, distilled water obtained from distillation of sea water is used for domestic purposes. Distilled water is mixed with groundwater to make it potable.

Activity 2

Aim: To demonstrate the separation of solid–liquid mixture using the method of distillation

Materials required: Round-bottomed flask, mixture (solution of salt and water), beaker, condenser, Bunsen burner and laboratory stands

Procedure: The apparatus is set up as shown in the figure.

1. Heat the mixture in the round-bottomed flask.
2. The mixture starts to boil and the liquid component (water) evaporates.
3. The vapours pass through the condenser, where they cool and condense to form the pure liquid that gets collected in the beaker.
4. The solid component (salt) is left behind.

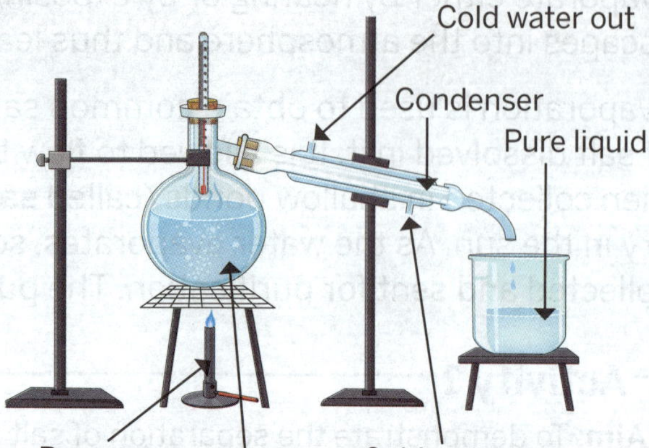

Observation: The liquid component is separated from the solid–liquid mixture leaving behind the solid component. The liquid thus obtained is in its pure form.

Conclusion: Distillation is used to obtain pure liquid from a solid–liquid mixture.

Separating Liquid–Liquid Mixtures

Separating Funnel

A separating funnel is used to separate a mixture of immiscible liquids.

Principle: This method is based on the principle that in immiscible liquids, the lighter liquid floats above the layer of the heavier liquid.

A separating funnel is a glass apparatus that is narrow at the bottom with a stopcock (like a tap). The funnel has an opening at the top to pour the liquid mixture. After the liquid mixture is poured, it is left undisturbed for some time. Immiscible liquids form separate layers with the heavier liquid at the bottom and the lighter liquid at the top. When the stopcock is opened, the heavier liquid at the bottom moves out first and is collected in a separate container. When the bottom layer flows out completely, the stopcock is closed. Only the lighter liquid remains in the separating funnel. Thus, the two liquids are separated.

A mixture of oil and water can be separated using this technique.

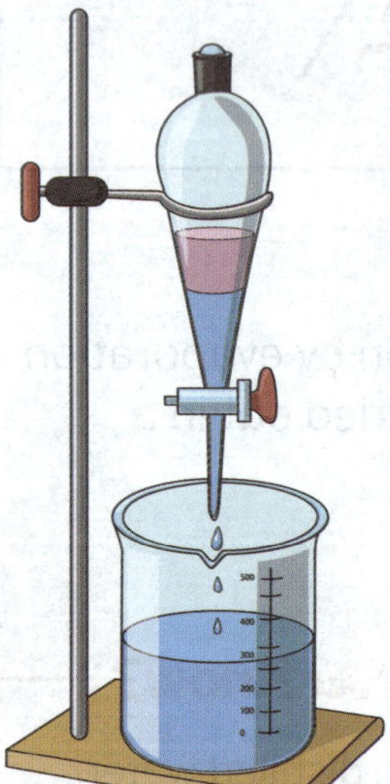

▲ Separation using a separating funnel

Fractional Distillation

Fractional distillation is the method used to separate a mixture of miscible liquids (liquids that can be mixed together completely).

Principle: This method is based on the difference in the boiling points of the liquid components to be separated.

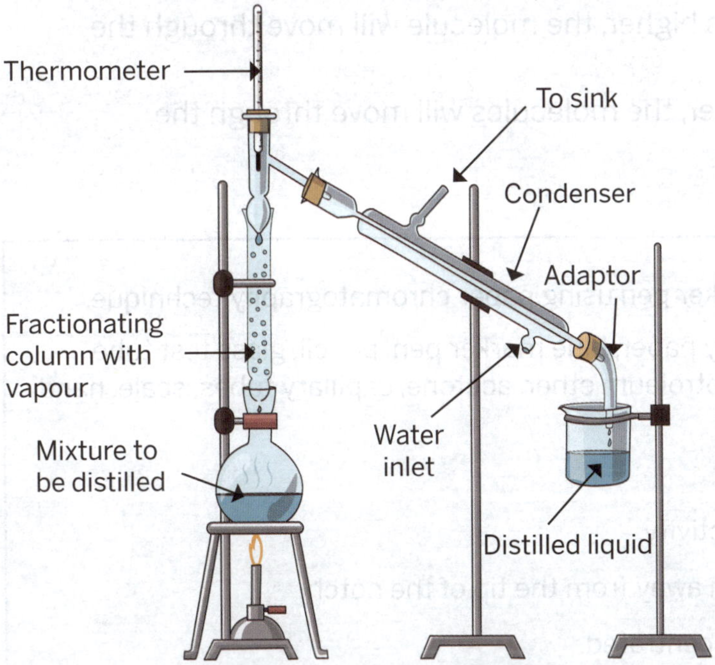

▲ Set-up of fractional distillation

The apparatus used for this method consists of a distillation flask, fractionating column, a condenser and heat supply. When a mixture of liquids is heated in the distillation flask, it boils and vapours rise up to the fractionating column. As the vapours go up in the column, the temperature inside the column begins to decrease. So, in the mixture, the liquid with a lower boiling point vaporizes first, rises to the top of the column and passes through the condenser. Here, the vapours cool down and condense to form a liquid which collects in a container. The vapours of the liquid with a higher boiling point condense and collect at the bottom of the fractionating column itself. Therefore, both the liquids boil at different temperatures and get collected.

This method is used to get petroleum products from crude oil, such as petrol, kerosene, diesel, gasoline, petroleum gas and tar.

Chromatography

It is a physical method of separation of mixture into individual components in which the components to be separated are distributed between two phases (the stationary phase and the mobile phase). Chromatography involves sample, stationary phase and mobile phase.

Paper Chromatography Principle: This technique is carried out using a particular kind of paper known as 'chromatographic paper'.

It is based on the difference in the rates of absorption of individual components of a mixture by this paper. The components of the solution to be separated start in one place on a strip of special paper. Solvents like water, acetone, petroleum ether, oil or isopropyl alcohol are allowed to absorb up the chromatographic paper strip. Various molecules will run up the chromatographic paper at different rates and the components of the solution get separated. This can be visible as strips of various colors on the chromatography paper.

Characteristics of stationary phase:

- Stationary phase is also known as 'adsorbent phase'.
- It is the substance that stays fixed inside the chromatography column.
- Stationary phase can be a liquid or a solid supported on a solid.

Characteristics of mobile phase:

- Mobile phase is also known as 'carrier phase'.
- It is the solvent that is moving through the chromatography column.
- Mobile phase can be a liquid or a gas.

- If the adsorption to the stationary phase is higher, the molecule will move through the chromatography column very slow.
- If the solubility in the mobile phase is higher, the molecules will move through the chromatography column very faster.

Activity 3

Aim: To separate the different colours of a marker pen using paper chromatography technique.

Materials required: Whatman chromatography paper, blue marker pen, pencil, glass test tube (boiling tube), measuring cylinder, split cork, petroleum ether, acetone, capillary tubes, scale, hand gloves, a pair of scissors and laboratory stand

Precautions:

- Wear hand gloves while performing the activity.
- The loading spot should be placed 2-3 cm away from the tip of the notch.
- The loading spot should be small and concentrated.
- The loading strip should remain 1 cm above the solvent level.
- The chromatographic strip should not touch the walls of the test tube.

Procedure:

1. Preparation of chromatography paper
   i. Take a narrow strip of chromatography paper.
   ii. Cut one end of the strip into a narrow notch with the help of scissors.
   iii. Draw a parallel line about 2 cm from the bottom.
2. Loading of the spot
   iv. Put a drop of the blue marker ink in the middle of the strip near the notch over the line with the help of a capillary tube.
   v. Allow the drop to dry and repeat till 4 or 5 ink drops are placed on the paper.
3. Set up of the chromatography paper
   vi. Take the test tube and pour about 5 ml of petroleum ether acetone solvent (in the ratio of 9:1) into the test tube.
   vii. Hang the chromatography strip in the test tube with the help of a split cork in such a way that the loading spot lies 1 cm above the solvent level.
   viii. Make the cork airtight and place the test tube undisturbed for some time.
   ix. Allow the chromatography paper to sit in the solvent until the solvent reaches the top line.
   x. Remove the chromatography paper and allow it to dry on a paper towel.

Observation and Conclusion: We can observe the rising up of the solvent in the chromatography paper dissolving the ink dye. The fully developed chromatography paper is known as a 'chromatogram'.

Explanation: The separation of the various colours of the ink mainly depends on two factors:

a. The property of the solutes to 'stick' to the chromatography paper, which is also known as 'adsorption'.

b. The property of the solutes to dissolve in the solvent.

These factors vary from substance to substance. Thus, we can infer that different substances will rise to different heights on the chromatography paper. Few dyes will stick to the chromatography paper very easily. Thus, as the solvent rises up, they will be left behind at various positions and can be separated easily.

Applications of chromatography

1. In isolation of plant pigments
   - Paper chromatography is a useful technique in the separation and identification of different plant pigments. The distance travelled by a particular plant pigment can be used to identify the compound.
2. In pharmaceutical industries
   - In pharmaceutical industries, chromatography is used for the synthesis of various drugs to check whether the product is synthesized from the reactants or not.
   - It is used to check the presence of any contamination in the manufactured compounds, using high performance liquid chromatography or gas chromatography.
3. In food industry
   - Chromatography is used in the determination of sugars in food samples.
   - It is used as a quality check in the food industry, in the process of analyzing and separating the additives, preservatives, amino acids and proteins.

Know the Scientist

Mikhail Tsvet (1872–1919) was a Russian–Italian botanist. He invented adsorption chromatography during his research on plant pigments. He used the technique to separate plant pigments such as chlorophylls, xanthophylls and carotenoids.

Revision Zone

Write T for True and F for False.

1. Evaporation is used to separate a mixture of milk and water.
2. The preferred method for separation of crude oil into its components is fractional distillation.
3. A separating funnel is used to separate plant pigments.
4. Only a particular kind of paper is used for chromatography technique.

Keywords

Element: a substance that consists of only one kind of atoms

Compound: a substance formed when two or more elements combine together chemically in a fixed ratio

Mixture: a substance that contains two or more different substances mixed together

Chemical symbol: the representation of an element using the short form or abbreviation of its name

Sublimation: the process in which a solid changes directly into its gaseous state without passing through its liquid state

Evaporation: the process in which a liquid changes into its gaseous state

Distillation: the method of separation of components of a mixture through evaporation and condensation

Fractional distillation: the process of separation of a mixture of miscible liquids based on the difference in their boiling points

Chromatography: the physical method of separation of mixture into individual components in which the components to be separated are distributed between stationary phase and mobile phase

In a Nutshell

- Pure substances consist of only one kind of atoms or molecules. Elements and compounds are examples of pure substances.
- Elements consist of only one kind of atoms.
- Chemical symbols are abbreviations used to denote elements.
- Two or more elements combine together chemically in a fixed ratio to form compounds.
- Two or more different substances (elements, compounds or both) mixed together to form mixtures.
- Mixtures can be classified into three types: solid–solid mixture, solid–liquid mixture and liquid–liquid mixture.
- Based on the distribution of components, mixtures can be classified as homogeneous and heterogeneous mixtures.
- The mixtures in which the components that make up the mixture are distributed uniformly and cannot be seen distinctly are called homogeneous mixtures. Examples are salt solution and bronze.
- The mixtures in which the components that make up the mixture are not distributed uniformly and can be seen distinctly are called heterogeneous mixtures. Examples are dust in air and oil in water.
- Mixtures can be separated using various methods like sublimation, evaporation, distillation, fractional distillation, using a separating funnel and chromatography.

Exercise

1. Choose the correct answer for each of the following.

a. The symbol of silver is

i. Hg ii. Sb

iii. Ag iv. S

b. Identify the chemical formula of calcium hydroxide.

i. CaOH ii. $Ca(OH)_2$

iii. Ca_2OH iv. $(Ca)_2OH$

c. Which of the following is used to separate two immiscible liquids?

i. Separating funnel

ii. Sublimation

iii. Filtration

iv. Evaporation

d. Sublimation can be used to separate a mixture of

i. sand and ammonium chloride

ii. sand and sugar

iii. iron fillings and salt

iv. stones and rice

e. Which of these is an example of homogeneous mixture?

i. Air

ii. Muddy water

iii. Oil in water

iv. Chalk powder in water

2. Fill in the blanks.

a. A substance that contains only one kind of atoms is called __________ (an element/a mixture).

b. The Latin name of sodium is __________ (*kalium/natrium*).

c. The chemical symbol of platinum is __________ (P/Pt).

d. Emulsion is an example of __________ (homogeneous/heterogeneous) mixture.

e. Compounds are __________ (pure/impure) substances.

3. Write T for True and F for False.

a. An alloy is an example of a mixture.

b. The valency of 1 should be written in the final formula of a compound.

c. The chemical formula represents one molecule of the compound.

d. Suspension is a mixture of two or more immiscible liquids.

e. The fully developed chromatography paper is known as a 'chromatogram'.

4. Define the following terms.

a. Element

b. Mixture

c. Chemical Symbol

d. Sublimation

e. Chromatography

f. Chemical formulae

5. Differentiate between the following.

a. Pure substance and mixture

b. Elements and compounds

c. Homogeneous mixtures and heterogeneous mixtures

d. Distillation and fractional distillation

e. Compounds and mixtures

6. Choose the odd one out. Give reasons for the choice.

a. Natrium, ferrum, cuprum, argon

b. Fe, Hg, Cu, Ca

c. Cu, MgO, Al, He

d. Iodine, camphor, sugar, ammonium chloride

e. Salt solution, sugar solution, honey, smoke

7 Answer the following questions in brief.

a. What is a pure substance? Give examples.

b. What is an element? Give any two characteristics.

c. What is the principle behind separating funnel method?

d. Why is distilled water the purest form of water? Give its uses.

e. Define chromatography and explain its principle.

8 Answer the following questions in detail.

a. Explain how elements got their symbols.

b. Write the features of the modern method of representing elements.

c. What are the steps involved in writing the chemical formula of magnesium chloride?

d. Following are the chemical formulae of some compounds. List the elements present and the number of atoms in each compound.

i. $CaCO_3$ ii. KNO_3

iii. H_2SO_4 iv. NaOH

e. Explain the method of distillation with the help of a diagram.

f. Describe the process of fractional distillation.

g. Explain how immiscible liquids are separated using a separating funnel.

9 Think and answer.

a. Helium (He), Neon (Ne) and Argon (Ar) do not have any valency. Why?

(Hint: Recall the concept of valency.)

b. An element A has valency 1 and an element B has valency 3. What would be the formula of the compound formed by A and B if B is a metal?

10 Project

- Take some chart papers and make game cards of various symbols and element names. Try to match the element cards with the relevant symbols.
- Visit a mineral water plant and find how water is purified before it is packed in bottles. Write a report on the whole process.

11 In the Library

Collect information about elements prepared in the lab synthetically and their inventors.

Worksheet

Subject Integration

a. Which of these below separation techniques is used in Kuwait to obtain clean water from the sea water for domestic purposes?

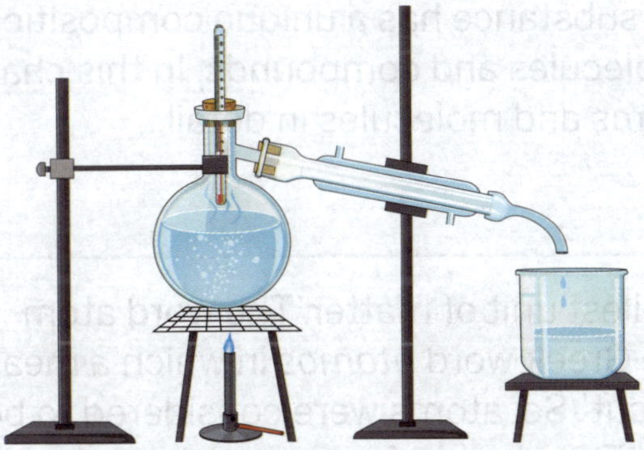

Separation Technique A

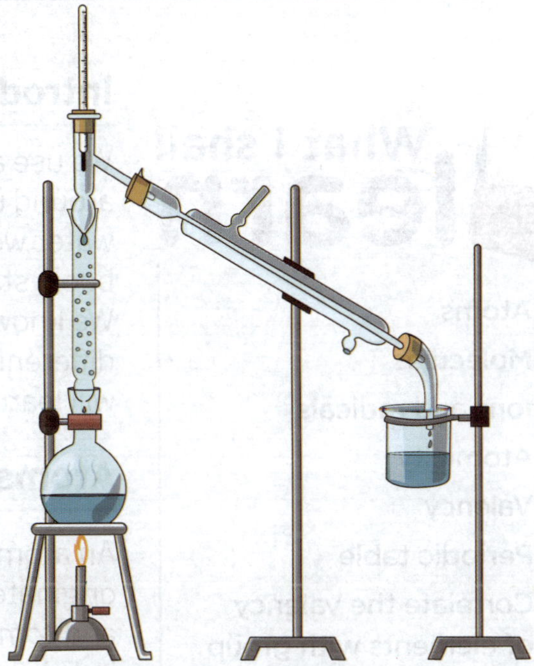

Separation Technique B

b. Name the separation techniques and their principle which are shown in the above images.

c. Do you think these separation techniques are used extensively in all geographical locations? If not, why do you think so?

Atomic Structure

4

What I shall learn

- Atoms
- Molecules
- Ions and radicals
- Atomicity
- Valency
- Periodic table
- Correlate the valency of elements with group number of periodic table

Introduction

We use a variety of substances in our daily life. Each substance around us is made of matter. For example, the food we eat, the water we drink, the air we breathe, non-living objects like table, book, stars and clouds, and living things are all made of matter. We know that each substance has a unique composition of different atoms, molecules and compounds. In this chapter, we will learn about atoms and molecules in detail.

Atoms

An atom is the smallest unit of matter. The word atom originated from the Greek word *atomos* in which *a* means 'not' and *tomos* means 'cut'. So, atoms were considered to be tiny, indivisible particles. The atoms of an element possess the properties of that element. An atom can either exist as a single atom (freely) or combine with atoms of the same element. Therefore, an **atom** can also be defined as the smallest particle of an element that exhibits all the properties of that element and may or may not exist independently.

The structure of an atom can be described as follows.

- The central part of an atom is called the **nucleus**, which is small and dense in nature. The positive charge of the atom and its mass is concentrated in the nucleus.

Science in Context

The nucleus of an atom is positive. But negative electrons do not fall into it. This is because the electrons have so much energy that they whirl around too fast to fall into the nucleus!

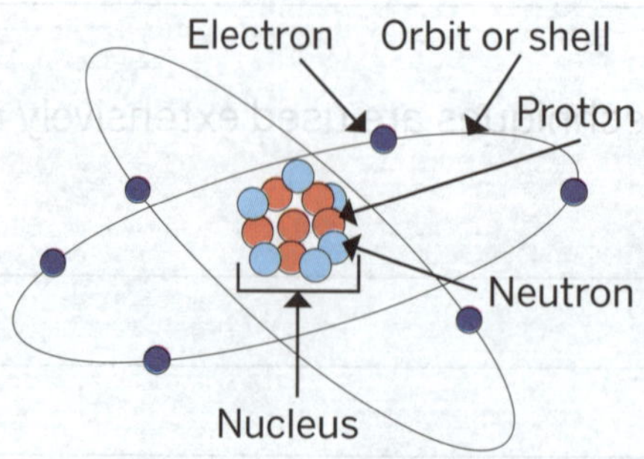

▲ Structure of an atom

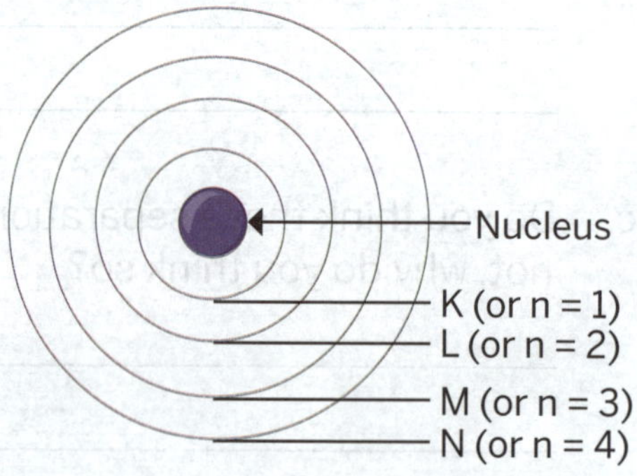

▲ Atomic model

- The **protons** (positively charged particles) and the **neutrons** (no charge/neutral particles) are present within the nucleus of an atom and are responsible for the mass of the atom.
- Outside the nucleus, the **electrons** (negatively charged particles) revolve around the nucleus in various fixed paths called **orbits** or **shells**. The electrons do not contribute to the mass of the atom.
- The number of electrons in an atom is equal to the number of protons present in its nucleus. So, the positive and negative charges cancel out, thus making the atom neutral in nature.
- The shells or orbits are represented by the numbers n = 1, 2, 3, 4 or by the letters K, L, M, N. These orbits or shells are also knows as 'energy levels' or 'energy shells'.
- The innermost energy shell (K-shell) that is closest to the nucleus has the lowest energy, the second energy shell (L-shell) has a higher energy than K-shell, and so on.
- Electrons lose energy when they move from a higher energy shell to a lower energy shell. On the other hand, electrons gain energy when they move from a lower energy shell to a higher energy shell.
- Each shell can accommodate only a fixed number of electrons. K-shell can hold 2 electrons, L-shell can hold 8 electrons, M-shell can hold 18 electrons and so on.
- The outermost shell of an atom is called its **valence shell**. The electrons in the valence shell determine the chemical reactivity of an atom and are called **valence electrons**. The valence shell can hold a maximum of eight electrons.

Do You Know?

Each energy shell is composed of one or more sub-shells with different energy levels. They are the s, p, d, and f sub-shells. These sub-shells accommodate only a fixed number of electrons: 2 electrons can be accommodated in the s sub-shell, 6 in p, 10 in d and 14 in f.

Revision Zone

Write T for True and F for False.

1. Each element has a name and a unique chemical symbol.
2. A neutron has mass equal to the mass of a proton.
3. Electrons revolve around the nucleus in fixed orbits.
4. The valence shell can hold a maximum of ten electrons.
5. Mass number is denoted by the letter Z.

Molecules

When two or more atoms of the same element or different elements combine, they form a molecule. The combining atoms are chemically bound or joined together to form molecules. A **molecule** can be defined as the smallest particle of an element or a compound that exhibits all the properties of that element or compound and can exist independently. Depending on whether a molecule is formed from atoms of same element or different elements, molecules are of two types: molecule of an element and molecule of a compound.

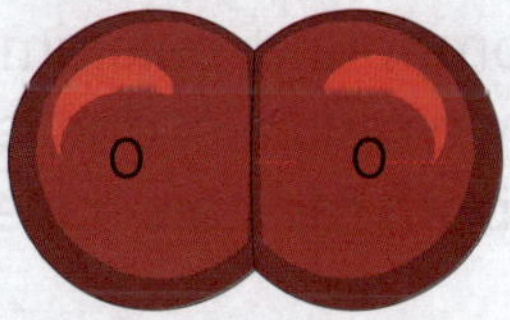

▲ Oxygen molecule (molecule of an element)

- When two or more atoms of the same element combine, a **molecule of an element** is formed. In molecules like oxygen (O_2) and chlorine (Cl_2), the same kind of atoms or atoms of the same element are bound together to form a molecule.

- When two or more atoms of different elements combine in a fixed proportion, a **molecule of a compound** is formed. In molecules like water (H_2O) and carbon dioxide (CO_2), different kinds of atoms or atoms of different elements are bound together to form a molecule.

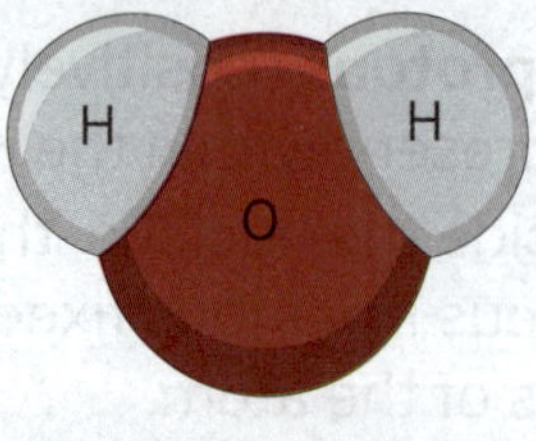

▲ Water molecule (molecule of a compound)

Ions and Radicals

Table 4.1 Some radicals and their symbols

Name of the radical	Symbol	Name of the radical	Symbol
Hydrogen	H^+	Hydride	H^-
Iron (II)	Fe^{2+}	Oxide	O^{2-}
Aluminium	Al^{3+}	Nitrate	NO_3^-
Magnesium	Mg^{2+}	Hydroxide	OH^-
Copper	Cu^{2+}	Hydrogen carbonate	HCO_3^-
Ammonium	NH_4^+	Phosphate	PO_4^{3-}

We studied that atoms are neutral (that is, they do not carry any charge) as the number of protons present inside the nucleus is equal to the number of electrons that revolve around the nucleus. However, when an atom donates or accepts one or more of electrons, this equality or balance is lost and the atom acquires a positive or negative charge. For example, when a sodium atom loses an electron, it acquires a positive charge (Na^+) as the number of protons in it becomes more than the number of electrons. Similarly, when a chlorine atom accepts an electron, it acquires a negative charge (Cl^-) as the number of electrons in it becomes more than the number of protons.

An atom that attains a negative or a positive charge as a result of loss or gain of electrons is called an **ion**. The atom that donates or loses electrons attains a positive charge and is called a **cation** or positive ion. Examples of cations are potassium (K^+), calcium (Ca^{2+}) and zinc (Zn^{2+}). The atom that accepts or gains electrons attains a negative charge and is called an **anion** or negative ion. Examples of anions are bromide (Br^-) , oxide (O^{2-}) and sulphide (S^{2-}).

An atom or a group of atoms of different elements that behaves as a single unit and carries a positive or negative charge is called a **radical**. A radical may contain one or more kinds of atoms. For example, zinc (Zn^{2+}) and sodium (Na^+) radicals contain only one kind of atoms; hence, these are called **simple radicals**. Carbonate (CO_3^{2-}) and sulphate (SO_4^{2-}) radicals contain two kinds of atoms each; hence, these are called **compound radicals**.

Radicals cannot exist independently and thus always combine with other radicals or elements. For example, carbonate is a compound radical with the formula CO_3^{2-}. It cannot exist independently and thus combines with other radicals like Ca^{2+} to form a compound, calcium carbonate ($CaCO_3$). The compound calcium carbonate ($CaCO_3$) contains two radicals: one is the positive radical Ca^{2+} and the other is the negative radical CO_3^{2-}, where both radicals have the valency 2.

Atomicity

Atoms of some elements exist independently or as a single atom. However, atoms of some elements cannot exist independently. So, atoms of such elements combine to form molecules which can exist independently.

The number of atoms that make up a molecule of an element is called its **atomicity**. The atomicity of an element is written on the right-hand side of the symbol as a subscript. Based on the number of atoms present, molecules can be called **monatomic** (containing only one atom), **diatomic** (containing two atoms), **triatomic** (containing three atoms) or **tetratomic** (containing four atoms). In general, molecules containing more than two atoms are called **polyatomic**.

Table 4.2 Atomicity of some elements

Element	Atomicity
Iron (Fe)	1 (Monatomic)
Aluminium (Al)	1 (Monatomic)
Argon (Ar)	1 (Monatomic)
Hydrogen (H_2)	2 (Diatomic)
Nitrogen (N_2)	2 (Diatomic)
Ozone (O_3)	3 (Triatomic)
Phosphorus (P_4)	4 (Tetratomic)
Sulphur (S_8)	8 (Polyatomic)

Valency

The combining capacity of an atom of an element with other atoms is known as its **valency**. It can also be defined as the number of electrons an atom can donate or accept in order to combine chemically with other atoms and form molecules.

We know that electrons revolve around the nucleus in orbits or shells. As electrons are present outside the nucleus, these are the only subatomic particles that take part in chemical reactions and help in forming different molecules. For instance, when two atoms combine together, one of the atoms donates or gives away one or more of its electrons and these electrons are accepted by the other atom. This results in the formation of a chemical bond between the two atoms which holds them together to form a molecule.

An atom is considered to be stable (or chemically inactive) if its valence or outermost shell is complete, that is, it has eight valence electrons. This implies that atoms having incomplete valence shells are chemically active or unstable. Therefore, in order to become stable, every atom whose valence shell is not complete tries to achieve a total of eight valence electrons by either donating or accepting electrons. For example, K atom has one electron in its outermost shell; so, it tends to lose this electron to achieve a total of eight valence electrons. However, Cl atom has seven electrons in its outermost shell; so, it tends to accept one electron to achieve a total of eight valence electrons.

Valency of an element is always a whole number. Depending upon the number of electrons the atom of an element can donate or accept, elements can be monovalent (valency 1), divalent (valency 2), trivalent (valency 3) or tetravalent (valency 4). Some elements and their valencies are given in Table 4.3.

Table 4.3 Some elements and their valencies

Element	Valency
Sodium	1 (Monovalent)
Chlorine	1 (Monovalent)
Hydrogen	1 (Monovalent)
Oxygen	2 (Divalent)
Calcium	2 (Divalent)
Magnesium	2 (Divalent)
Aluminium	3 (Trivalent)
Carbon	4 (Tetravalent)

Elements of metals tend to donate electrons as they have 1, 2 or 3 electrons in their valence shell. So, by donating these valence electrons, metals acquire stability. On the other hand, elements of non-metals tend to accept electrons as they have 5, 6 or 7 electrons in their valence shell. So, they accept electrons to complete their valence shell and thus acquire stability.

Variable Valency

Some elements exhibit more than one valency as their atoms have different combining capacities while forming molecules or compounds. That is, atoms of such elements can donate or accept different number of electrons depending upon the conditions. Hence, we can say that these elements have variable valencies. For example, copper can have variable valencies of 1 and 2. In cuprous chloride ($CuCl$), the valency of copper is 1, whereas in cupric chloride ($CuCl_2$), its valency is 2. Elements with variable valencies are represented by writing the symbol of the element followed by its valency in Roman numerals within brackets.

Table 4.4 Variable valencies of some elements

Element	Variable valencies	Representation
Copper	1, 2	Cu (I), Cu (II)
Iron	2, 3	Fe (II), Fe (III)
Silver	1, 2	Ag (I), Ag (II)
Mercury	1, 2	Hg (I), Hg (II)
Nickel	2, 3, 4	Ni (II), Ni (III), Ni (IV)

Revision Zone

Match the compounds with their valencies.

1. Aluminium	a. Monovalent
2. Magnesium	b. Tetravalent
3. Chlorine	c. Divalent
4. Carbon	d. Trivalent

Periodic Table

Mendeleev's periodic table was the first classification that successfully accommodated the available elements. It was limited to 63 elements and they were arranged in the periodic table based on the increasing order of their atomic masses.

- The modern classification of the elements was applicable to 118 elements and these elements are arranged in the periodic table based on their atomic number.
- The elements are arranged in horizontal rows called 'periods' and vertical columns called 'groups'. There are 7 periods and 18 groups in the periodic table.
- All the elements in a group show regular gradation of the physical properties and similar chemical reactivities.
- All the elements in a period show regular gradation of the properties (increase or decrease) from left to right.

Periodic Table of Elements

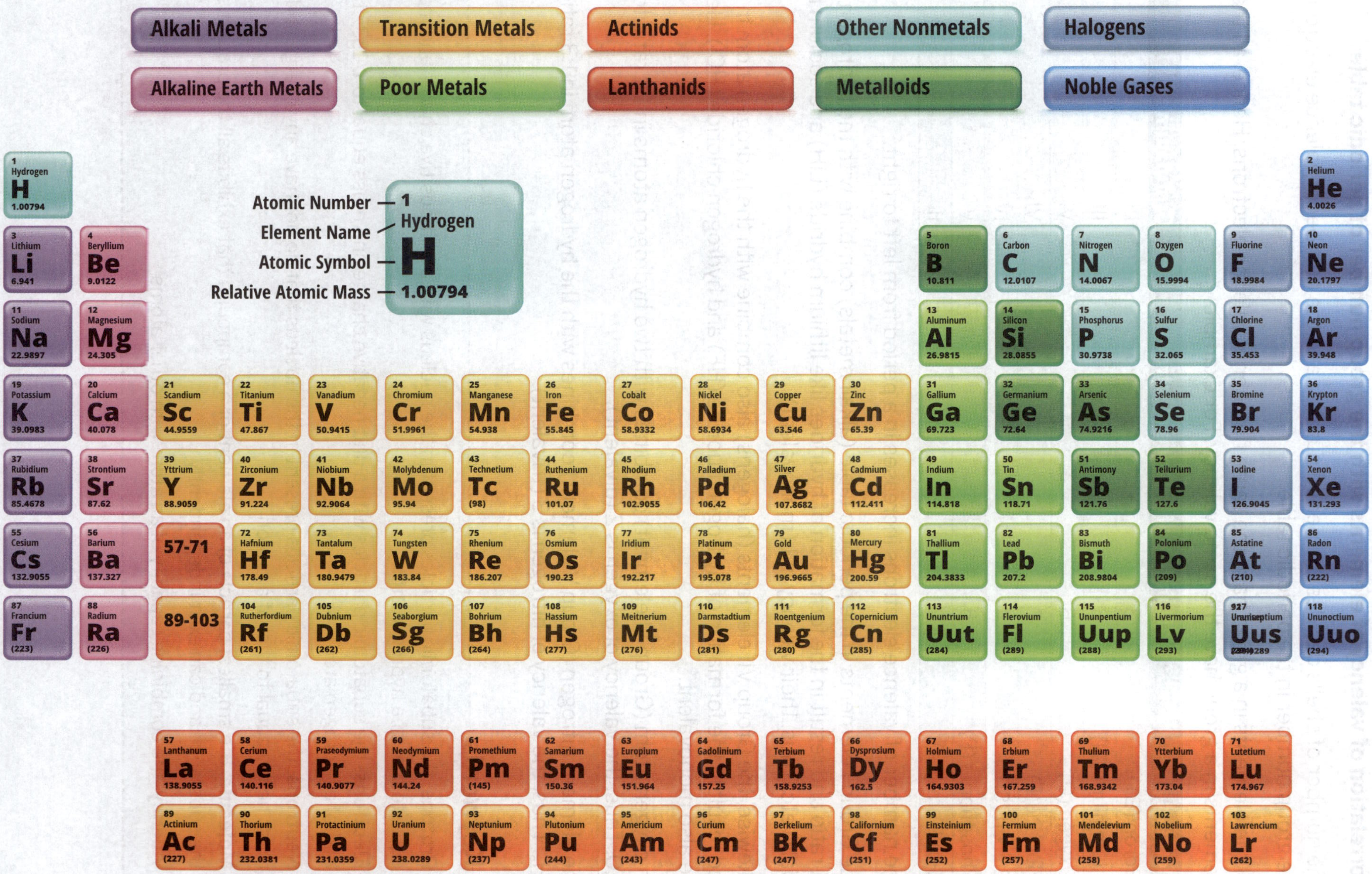

Correlation of valency of elements with the group number of periodic table

The number of shells decides the period number and the number of valence electrons decides the group number in the periodic table.

All the elements in a group have the same number of valence electrons. Hence, all the elements in a group have the same valency. For example:

Element	Number of valence electrons	Group number
Boron (B)	3	III
Aluminium (Al)	3	III
Oxygen (O)	6	VI
Fluorine(F)	7	VII
Silicon (Si)	4	IV
Phosphorus (P)	5	V
Beryllium (Be)	2	II

The number of valence electrons increases in a period from left to right.

The Group I elements in the periodic table (alkali metals) combine with the hydrogen atom in 1:1 ratio and result in the formation of hydrides like lithium hydride (LiH) and sodium hydride (NaH) etc. Thus, their valency is 1 (monovalent).

Likewise, the Group VII elements (halogens) also combine with the hydrogen atom in 1:1 ratio and result in the formation of hydrogen fluoride (HF) and hydrogen chloride (HCl). Hence, they are also monovalent.

An oxygen atom (Group VI element) combines with two hydrogen atoms in 1:2 ratio to form H_2O. Thus, the valency of oxygen is 2 (divalent).

The element nitrogen (Group V element) combines with the hydrogen atom in 1:3 ratio to form NH_3. Thus, the valency of nitrogen is 3 (trivalent).

Keywords

Protons: the subatomic particles present in the nucleus with a unit positive charge and mass equal to that of a hydrogen atom

Electrons: the subatomic particles with a unit negative charge and mass equal to 1/1837 times that of a hydrogen atom

Neutrons: the subatomic particles present in the nucleus that do not have any charge and have mass nearly equal to that of a proton

Molecule: the smallest particle of an element or a compound that exhibits all the properties of the substance and can exist independently

Valency: the combining capacity of an atom with other atoms

In a Nutshell

- An atom is the smallest unit of matter. The word atom is derived from the Greek word *atomos* which means indivisible.
- The protons, electrons and neutrons are the fundamental particles of an atom.
- The nucleus is the central part of an atom in which all the positive charge of the atom and the mass of the atom is concentrated in a small volume.
- Ions are the atoms that attain negative or positive charge due to gain or loss of electrons.
- The atom that donates or loses electrons attains a positive charge and is called a cation.
- The atom that accepts or gains electrons attains a negative charge and is called an anion.
- Radical is an atom or a group of atoms of different elements that behaves as a single unit and carries a positive or negative charge.
- The elements are arranged in horizontal rows called periods and vertical columns called groups. There are 7 periods and 18 groups in the periodic table.
- The number of shells decides the period number and the number of valence electrons decides the group number in the periodic table.

Exercise

1 Choose the correct option from the following.

a. The nucleus of an atom consists of
   i. neutrons and protons
   ii. electrons and neutrons
   iii. electrons and neutrons
   iv. electrons, protons and neutrons

b. Identify the triatomic element from the following.
   i. Nitrogen ii. Ozone
   iii. Phosphorus iv. Argon

c. Which of the following is a divalent element?
   i. Aluminium ii. Sodium
   iii. Magnesium iv. Carbon

d. The valency of oxygen is
   i. 1 ii. 2
   iii. 3 iv. 4

e. Which of the following elements shows variable valency?
   i. Nickel ii. Sodium
   iii. Helium iv. Carbon

f. Identify the negative radical from the following.
   i. Aluminium ii. Hydroxide
   iii. Magnesium iv. Ammonium

2 Fill in the blanks using the correct words.

a. A substance that contains only one kind of atoms is called ________ (an element/a mixture).

b. Subatomic particles with a negative charge are called ________ (electrons/protons).

c. The element phosphorus is ________ (diatomic/tetratomic).

d. An atom with a negative charge is called ________ (a cation/an anion).

e. The elements are arranged in horizontal rows called ________ (groups/periods).

3 Write T for True and F for False.

a. Neutrons do not have any charge.

b. Chlorine is a divalent element.

c. Copper exhibits variable valency.

d. Cations are atoms that have a positive charge.

e. In an ionic bond, two atoms share electrons.

4 Define the following terms.

a. Atomicity

b. Valency

c. Protons

d. Neutrons

e. Electrons

f. Element

5 Differentiate between the following.

a. Atom and molecule

b. Protons and electrons

c. Cation and anion

d. Simple radicals and compound radicals

e. Groups and periods

6 Answer the following questions in brief.

a. What is an element? Give any two characteristics.

b. What are subatomic particles of an atom? Name them.

c. Where are electrons found in an atom?

d. What are valence electrons? What is their importance?
e. What is a polyatomic molecule? Give examples.
f. What is variable valency? Give an example.
g. What is a radical?
h. Write a note on periodic table.

7 Answer the following questions in detail.

a. Explain the structure of an atom with a diagram.
b. What is the difference between an ion and a radical? Mention any five radicals and their symbols.
c. Explain the correlation between valencies with the group number in the periodic table.

8 Think and answer.

a. Helium (He), Neon (Ne) and Argon (Ar) do not have any valency. Why? (Hint: Recall the concept of valency.)
b. An element A has valency 1 and an element B has valency 3. What would be the formula of the compound formed by A and B if B is a metal?

9 Project

Take some chart papers and make game cards of various symbols, element names and valencies. Try to match the element cards with the relevant symbols and valencies.

10 In the Library

Collect information about the history of atoms and prepare a timeline of it on a chart paper. Discuss with your teacher and display the same on your school notice board.

Subject Integration

a. Draw a labelled diagram depicting the structure of an atom.

b. We know that the nucleus of an atom is positively charged and the electrons that revolve around the nucleus are negatively charged. Electrons being negative do not fall into the nucleus of an atom. Why is it so? Write your answer in the space provided.

c. You might have experienced small shocks when we touch metallic door knobs or metallic water taps during dry days. There is no electric current flowing through the door knob or water tap. Then, how do we get those shocks?

Language of Chemistry

5

What I shall learn

- Chemical reactions
- Characteristics of chemical reactions
- Chemical equations

Introduction

We observe various types of changes that take place around us. For example, change in the weather, the occurrence of day and night, melting of wax, freezing of water, rotting of vegetables, salt or sugar getting dissolved in water, ripening of fruits and rusting of iron.

A **change** can be defined as the transformation of substance from one form to another. Changes can be broadly classified into two types: physical changes and chemical changes. Changes in which no new substances are formed are known as **physical changes**. Changes in which new substances are formed are known as **chemical changes**. We know that when a chemical change takes place, new products are formed that have properties different from the original substance. This is because of the chemical reactions that take place during a chemical change. Let us learn more about chemical reactions.

Chemical Reactions

We know that when a chemical change takes place, new products are formed that have properties different from the original substance. This is because of the chemical reactions that take place during a chemical change. A chemical change in which two or more substances (elements or compounds) react or combine to form one or more new substances (elements or compounds) or one substance decomposes in to two or more substances is called a **chemical reaction**.

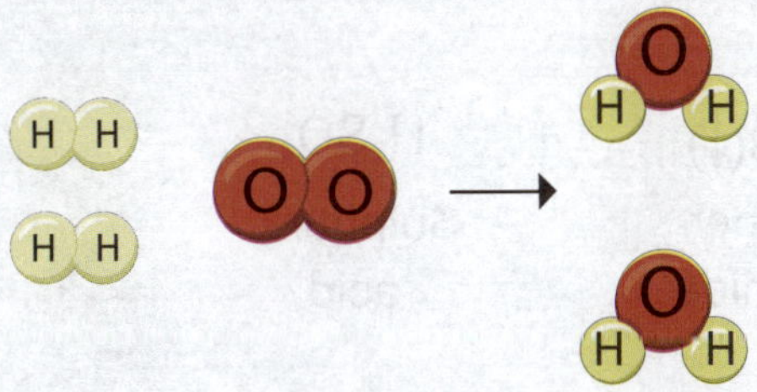

$$2H_2 + O_2 \longrightarrow 2H_2O$$

▲ Chemical reaction between hydrogen and oxygen

In a chemical reaction, atoms in the molecules of the original substance(s) rearrange themselves to form one or more new products or substances.

Consider the example of formation of water. It involves the reaction of two molecules of hydrogen (that is, 4 atoms of hydrogen) with one molecule of oxygen (that is, 2 atoms of oxygen) to form two molecules of water. In this reaction, we can see that no new elements or atoms are formed. Four atoms of hydrogen and two atoms of oxygen rearrange themselves and form two molecules of water with the help of chemical bonds. Therefore, before and after the chemical reaction (or chemical change), the total number of atoms of each kind in the original substances and in the new product remains the same.

During a chemical reaction, either two or more elements or compounds react with each other to form new compounds, or a compound splits into two or more elements or compounds.

Characteristics of Chemical Reactions

Chemical reactions may also exhibit one or more of the following characteristics.

- **Change in colour**: Some chemical reactions show a change in the colour of the reactants, that is, the colour of the product may differ from that of the reactants.

  For example, copper sulphate solution is blue in colour. When an iron nail is dropped into the solution, the blue colour slowly changes into a light green colour. This happens because of the chemical reaction that takes place between copper sulphate and iron resulting in the formation of iron sulphate, which is green in colour.

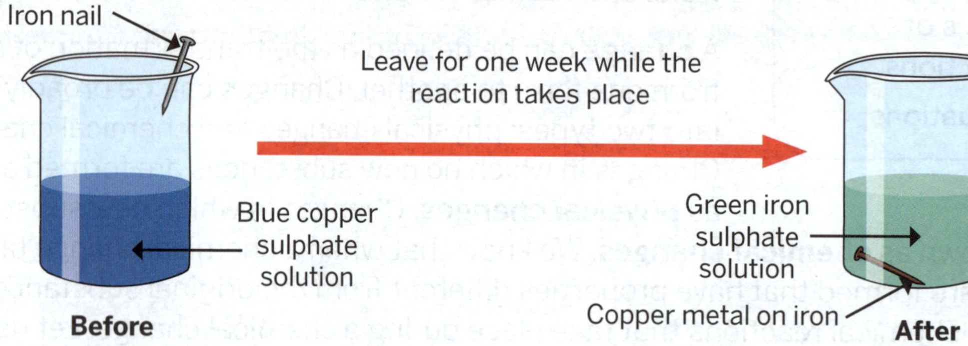

▲ Change in colour is one of the characteristics of chemical reactions

Fe	+	$CuSO_4$	$\longrightarrow$	$FeSO_4$	+	Cu
Iron		Copper sulphate (Blue)		Iron sulphate (Green)		Copper

- **Formation of precipitate**: In some chemical reactions, the product formed separates from the solution and forms a different mass or layer. This insoluble solid is called a **precipitate**.

  For example, in a reaction between copper sulphate solution and hydrogen sulphide gas, copper sulphide and sulphuric acid are formed. The copper sulphide formed is given out as a black precipitate.

$CuSO_4$	+	H_2S	$\longrightarrow$	$CuS(\downarrow)$	+	H_2SO_4
Copper sulphate		Hydrogen sulphide		Copper sulphide		Sulphuric acid

Activity 1

Aim: To observe the colour change and the formation of precipitate in the reaction between potassium iodide and lead acetate.

Materials required: Test tube, potassium iodide, lead acetate

Procedure:

- Take potassium iodide (KI) in a glass test tube.
- Slowly add lead acetate [$Pb(CH_3COO)_2$] solution into it.
- Gently shake the contents of the test tube and observe.

Observation: The colour of the solution in the test tube changes to yellow and formation of a yellow-coloured precipitate is observed in the test tube.

Conclusion: The yellow-coloured precipitate formed in the test tube is due to the formation of a new product lead iodide.

$$Pb(CH_3COO)_2 + 2KI \rightarrow PbI_2 + 2CH_3COOK$$

Lead acetate + Potassium iodide → Lead iodide (↓) + Potassium acetate

- **Evolution of gas**: During some chemical reactions, gases are produced. These gases are actually the products formed in the gaseous state. Gases thus evolved can be identified by carrying out some simple chemical tests on them. For example, when sodium bicarbonate (baking soda) reacts with acetic acid (vinegar), carbon dioxide gas is evolved in the form of brisk effervescence (that is, seen as bubbles in the liquid).

$$NaHCO_3 + CH_3COOH \longrightarrow CH_3COONa + H_2O + CO_2(\uparrow)$$

Sodium bicarbonate + Acetic acid ⟶ Sodium acetate + Water + Carbon dioxide

The presence of carbon dioxide can be confirmed by passing it through lime water as it turns lime water milky. Similarly, the presence of hydrogen gas can be confirmed as it burns with a pop sound when a burning splint is brought near it.

Some gases have a distinct odour and thus can be easily identified. For example, ammonia (NH_3) gas has a very pungent odour.

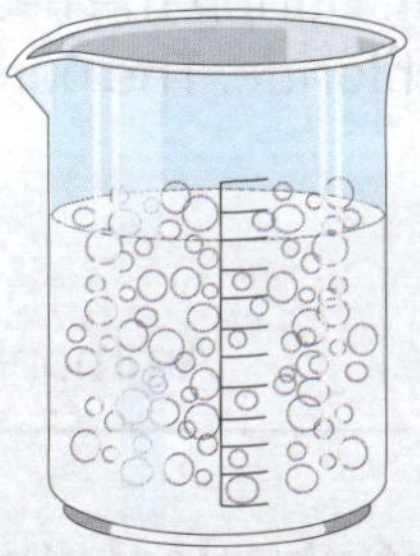

▲ Evolution of carbon dioxide gas during the chemical reaction between vinegar and baking soda

- **Change of smell**: Some chemical changes may result in the change of smell or odour due to the formation of new products. Hence, change of smell/odour is considered as one of the characteristics to recognize the chemical change.

Activity 2

Aim: To observe the evolution of gas during the reaction between sodium carbonate and hydrochloric acid

***Note**: To be demonstrated by the teacher*

Materials required: Test tube, sodium carbonate, dilute hydrochloric acid, lime water

Procedure:

- Take sodium carbonate (Na_2CO_3) in a glass test tube.
- Slowly add dilute hydrochloric acid (HCl) solution into the test tube.
- Gently shake the contents of the test tube and observe.

Observation: Brisk effervescence will be observed in the test tube.

Conclusion: Brisk effervescence is observed due to the release of carbon dioxide gas during the chemical reaction between sodium carbonate and hydrochloric acid.

$$2HCl + Na_2CO_3 \rightarrow 2NaCl + CO_2 \uparrow + H_2O$$

The release of carbon dioxide gas during this chemical reaction can be verified by passing CO_2 gas into a test tube containing lime water. Carbon dioxide gas turns the lime water into milky.

Activity 3

Aim: To observe the evolution of gas and smell during the heating process of ammonium chloride

Materials required: Test tube, ammonium chloride, Bunsen burner

Procedure:

- Take ammonium chloride in a glass test tube.
- Carefully heat the contents of the test tube over Bunsen burner and observe.

Observation: Release of colourless fumes with a pungent odour will be observed.

Conclusion: During the heating of ammonium chloride, it decomposes into ammonia gas and hydrogen chloride. The pungent odour during this reaction is due to the formation of ammonia (NH_3) gas.

$$NH_4Cl + Heat \rightarrow NH_3 (\uparrow) + HCl$$

Ammonium chloride + Heat → Ammonia + Hydrogen chloride

- **Change of physical state**: Some chemical reactions may result in a change of physical state from reactants to products.

  For example, when solid zinc reacts with hydrochloric acid, it forms zinc chloride, which is in a liquid state, and releases hydrogen gas.

$$\underset{\text{Zinc}}{Zn(s)} + \underset{\text{Hydrochloric acid}}{2HCl(l)} \longrightarrow \underset{\text{Zinc chloride}}{ZnCl_2 (aq)} + \underset{\text{Hydrogen}}{H_2(\uparrow)}$$

- **Change of energy**: Chemical reactions generally involve a change of energy during the course of the reaction. Energy is either absorbed or liberated during a chemical reaction and it is mostly in the form of heat and light. In some cases, sound is also produced. Based on whether heat energy is absorbed or liberated, chemical reactions are of two types.

  i. **Endothermic reactions**: Chemical reactions in which heat energy is absorbed from the surroundings are called **endothermic reactions.** For example, when carbon and sulphur are heated together, carbon disulphide is formed.

  $$\underset{\text{Carbon}}{C} + \underset{\text{Sulphur}}{2S} + \text{Heat} \longrightarrow \underset{\text{Carbon disulphide}}{CS_2}$$

  When calcium carbonate is heated to a high temperature, calcium oxide and carbon dioxide are produced.

  $$\underset{\text{Calcium carbonate}}{CaCO_3} \xrightarrow{\text{Heat}} \underset{\text{Calcium oxide}}{CaO} + \underset{\text{Carbon dioxide}}{CO_2}$$

  ii. **Exothermic reactions**: Chemical reactions in which heat energy is liberated are called **exothermic reactions**. For example, when carbon burns in the presence of oxygen, carbon dioxide is formed along with the generation of heat.

  $$\underset{\text{Carbon}}{C} + \underset{\text{Oxygen}}{O_2} \longrightarrow \underset{\text{Carbon dioxide}}{CO_2} + \text{Heat}$$

  Other examples of exothermic reactions are respiration, burning of fuels like coal, petrol and kerosene, and rusting.

Do You Know?

When we apply nail polish remover, we get a cooling effect on our finger nails and toe nails. This is because the acetone present in the nail polish remover absorbs heat from our body while evaporating.

Activity 4

Aim: To observe the liberation of heat in the reaction between HCl and NaOH

Materials required: Test tube, sodium hydroxide pellets, hydrochloric acid

Procedure:

- Take few pellets of sodium hydroxide (NaOH) in a glass test tube.
- Slowly add hydrochloric acid solution (HCl) into the test tube.
- Gently shake the contents of the test tube and carefully touch the sides of the glass test tube

Observation: Heat can be felt when we touch the sides of the test tube.

Conclusion: During the chemical reaction between hydrochloric acid and sodium hydroxide, energy is liberated in the form of heat .This reaction is exothermic reaction as heat energy is released.

$$HCl + NaOH \rightarrow NaCl + H_2O + \text{Heat}$$

Hydrogen chloride + Sodium hydroxide → Sodium chloride + Water + Heat

Science in Context

The process in which the surface of cut fruits and vegetables turns brown is called **browning**. It is an example of a **chemical change**.

We can prevent the browning process from taking place by keeping the cut vegetables and fruits immersed in water. The water prevents the air from coming in contact with the vegetables and fruits, thus preventing the browning process.

Chemical Equations

We have learned in the previous chapter that symbols are used to represent elements, while chemical formulae are used to represent compounds. Similarly, a chemical reaction can also be represented using symbols and formulae.

The representation of a chemical reaction using the symbols and formulae of the elements or compounds involved in the reaction is known as a **chemical equation**.

A chemical reaction can also be expressed in words, that is, by writing only the names of the elements or compounds involved in the reaction. The equation is then known as a **word equation**. Let us look at the reaction of hydrogen and chlorine to form hydrogen chloride.

Word equation: Hydrogen + Chlorine ⟶ Hydrogen chloride

Chemical equation: $H_2 + Cl_2 \longrightarrow 2HCl$

Characteristics of a Chemical Equation

The characteristics of a chemical equation are as follows:

- A chemical equation consists of reactants and products.

  The chemical substances that participate in a chemical reaction are known as **reactants**.

  The new substances formed due to a chemical reaction are known as **products**.
- It gives information about the number of reactants taking part and products being formed.

For example, consider the reaction of hydrogen with chlorine.

$$H_2 + Cl_2 \longrightarrow 2HCl$$

Here, one hydrogen molecule reacts with one chlorine molecule to form two molecules of hydrogen chloride. In this reaction, hydrogen and chlorine are reactants while hydrogen chloride is the product formed.

Writing Chemical Equations

Following are the steps to write a chemical equation.

1. The reactants are written on the left-hand side (LHS) and the combination is shown with a plus sign (+) between them.
2. The products are written on the right-hand side (RHS). If there is more than one product, then a plus sign is written between the two products.

3. In between the reactants and the products, an arrow is placed. The head of the arrow points towards the products, which denotes the direction or flow of the reaction.
4. If a chemical reaction has any necessary conditions for it to take place, then these are written either above or below the arrow.

Let us consider the reaction of calcium with oxygen and write its chemical equation. Calcium reacts with oxygen to form calcium oxide. The word equation of this chemical reaction would be:

$$\text{Calcium} + \text{Oxygen} \longrightarrow \text{Calcium oxide}$$

To write a chemical equation, the names of the reactants and the products are replaced with their symbols and formulae.

$$Ca + O_2 \longrightarrow CaO$$

$$\underbrace{\text{Calcium (Ca)} + \text{Oxygen } (O_2)}_{\text{(Reactants)}} \longrightarrow \underbrace{\text{Calcium oxide (CaO)}}_{\text{(Product)}}$$

The number of atoms of each element on both sides of the chemical equation should be equal, that is, the equation should be balanced. Let us now learn how to balance an equation.

Balancing Chemical Equations

Consider the chemical reaction of calcium with oxygen discussed above.

$$Ca + O_2 \longrightarrow CaO$$

1. Count the number of atoms of each element in the reactants and the products of the chemical equation.

Element	Number of atoms in reactants (LHS)	Number of atoms in products (RHS)
Ca	1	1
O	2	1

From the table, we can see that one atom of calcium and two atoms of oxygen take part in the reaction to form one molecule of calcium oxide. But one oxygen atom is enough to react with calcium to form one molecule of calcium oxide. The remaining oxygen atom cannot be destroyed. So, if there are two oxygen atoms participating in a reaction, each will need a calcium atom. So, we balance the equation to show the correct number of atoms participating in the reaction. Let us see how we can do that.

2. To balance the oxygen atoms on both sides of the equation, multiply the product (RHS) by 2.

$$\underset{\text{Calcium}}{Ca} + \underset{\text{Oxygen}}{O_2} \longrightarrow \underset{\text{Calcium oxide}}{2CaO}$$

Element	LHS	RHS
Ca	1	1×2=2
O	2	1×2=2

Now in the equation, the number of oxygen atoms is balanced but the number of calcium atoms on both sides is not balanced.

3. To balance the calcium atoms on both sides of the equation, multiply the number of calcium atoms in the reactants (LHS) by 2.

$$\underset{\text{Calcium}}{2Ca} + \underset{\text{Oxygen}}{O_2} \longrightarrow \underset{\text{Calcium oxide}}{2CaO}$$

Element	LHS	RHS
Ca	1×2=2	1×2=2
O	2	1×2=2

Now, the above chemical equation is said to be balanced.

A chemical equation in which the number of atoms of each element on both sides of the equation (i.e., the reactants and the products) is equal is known as a **balanced chemical equation**. A chemical equation in which the number of atoms of each element on both sides of the equation (i.e., the reactants and the products) is not equal is known as an **unbalanced chemical equation**. An unbalanced chemical equation is also called a **skeletal equation**.

A chemical equation is balanced to equalize the number of atoms of each element in the reactants and the products. According to the **Law of Conservation of Mass**, atoms are neither created nor destroyed. Hence, during a chemical reaction, the atoms are only rearranged to provide new products. The rearrangement of atoms happens in such a way that the total mass of the reactants is equal to the total mass of the products. That is, the number of atoms of each element in the reactants and the products remains the same.

We can get the following information by looking at a balanced chemical equation:

- The reactants that take part in the reaction and the products that are formed
- The number of molecules of the reactants and the products that take part in the reaction
- The number of atoms of each element of the reactants and the products that take part in the reaction
- Help in determining the mass of the reactants and the products that take part in the reaction

Let us look at some examples of balancing chemical equations.

Balancing Chemical Equations

Example 1: Mercury reacts with oxygen to form mercuric oxide.

$$Hg + O_2 \longrightarrow HgO$$

Step 1: Count the number of atoms of each element in the reactants and the products.

Element	LHS	RHS
Hg	1	1
O	2	1

In this reaction, one atom of mercury reacts with two atoms of oxygen to form one molecule of mercuric oxide. The number of mercury atoms in the reactants and the product is balanced. But the oxygen atoms are not balanced. So, we need to balance the equation.

Step 2: To balance the oxygen atoms, multiply HgO in the product by 2.

$$Hg + O_2 \longrightarrow 2HgO$$

Now, the number of mercury atoms on both sides of the equation is not balanced. Hence, it should be balanced.

Element	LHS	RHS
Hg	1	$1\times2=2$
O	2	$1\times2=2$

Step 3: To balance the mercury atoms, multiply the number of mercury atoms in the reactants by 2.

$$2Hg + O_2 \longrightarrow 2HgO$$

The equation is now said to be balanced.

Element	LHS	RHS
Hg	$1\times2=2$	$1\times2=2$
O	2	$1\times2=2$

Example 2: Potassium chlorate on heating splits to form potassium chloride and oxygen.

$$KClO_3 \longrightarrow KCl + O_2$$

Step 1: Count the number of atoms of each element in the reactants and the products.

Element	LHS	RHS
K	1	1
Cl	1	1
O	3	2

The number of potassium and chlorine atoms in both the reactant and the products is balanced. But the oxygen atoms are not balanced. Hence, we need to balance the equation.

Step 2: To balance the oxygen atoms, multiply $KClO_3$ in the reactant by 2 and the oxygen atoms in the products by 3.

$$2KClO_3 \longrightarrow KCl + 3O_2$$

Element	LHS	RHS
K	$1\times2=2$	1
Cl	$1\times2=2$	1
O	$3\times2=6$	$2\times3=6$

The number of oxygen atoms is balanced, but the number of potassium and chlorine atoms on both sides of the equation is not balanced.

Step 3: To balance the potassium and the chlorine atoms, multiply KCl in the products by 2.

$$2KClO_3 \longrightarrow 2KCl + 3O_2$$

Element	LHS	RHS
K	2	$1\times2=2$
Cl	2	$1\times2=2$
O	6	6

The equation is now said to be balanced.

Example 3: Calcium reacts with water to form calcium hydroxide and hydrogen.

$$Ca + H_2O \longrightarrow Ca(OH)_2 + H_2$$

Element	LHS	RHS
Ca	1	1
H	2	4
O	1	2

Step 1: Count the number of atoms of each element in the reactants and the products.

The number of calcium atoms on both sides of the equation is balanced. But the hydrogen and the oxygen atoms are not balanced.

Step 2: To balance the hydrogen and the oxygen atoms, multiply the hydrogen and the oxygen atoms in the reactants by 2.

$$Ca + 2H_2O \longrightarrow Ca(OH)_2 + H_2$$

Element	LHS	RHS
Ca	1	1
H	$2\times2=4$	4
O	$1\times2=2$	2

The number of hydrogen and oxygen atoms on both sides of the equation is now balanced. Hence, the equation is said to be balanced.

Example 4: Iron sulphide reacts with hydrobromic acid to form iron bromide and hydrogen sulphide.

$$FeS + HBr \longrightarrow FeBr_2 + H_2S$$

Element	LHS	RHS
Fe	1	1
S	1	1
H	1	2
Br	1	2

Step 1: Count the number of atoms of each element in the reactants and the products.

The number of iron and sulphur atoms is balanced, but the number of hydrogen and bromine atoms is not balanced on both sides of the equation.

Step 2: To balance the hydrogen and the bromine atoms, multiply the hydrogen and the bromine atoms in the reactants by 2.

$$FeS + 2HBr \longrightarrow FeBr_2 + H_2S$$

Element	LHS	RHS
Fe	1	1
S	1	1
H	$1 \times 2 = 2$	2
Br	$1 \times 2 = 2$	2

Now, the number of hydrogen and bromine atoms on both sides of the equation is balanced. Thus, the equation is said to be balanced.

Revision Zone

Balance the following chemical equations.

1. ______ Cu + ______ O_2 $\longrightarrow$ ______ CuO
2. ______ Ca + ______ H_2O $\longrightarrow$ ______ $Ca(OH)_2$ + H_2
3. ______ KOH + ______ H_2SO_4 $\longrightarrow$ ______ K_2SO_4 + ______ H_2O
4. ______ Fe + ______ O_2 $\longrightarrow$ ______ Fe_2O_3

Keywords

Chemical changes: changes in which new substances are formed

Chemical reaction: a chemical change in which two or more substances react or combine to form one or more new substances or one substance decomposes into two or more substances

Chemical equation: the representation of a chemical reaction using symbols and formulae

Endothermic reactions: chemical reactions in which heat is absorbed

Exothermic reactions: chemical reactions in which heat is evolved

Physical changes: changes in which no new substances are formed

Products: the new substances formed during a chemical reaction

Reactants: the chemical substances that participate in a chemical reaction

In a Nutshell

- Change is the conversion of any substance from one form to another.
- Changes in which no new substances are formed are known as physical changes. Some examples are folding of a paper, cutting of an iron rod into pieces and melting of butter.
- Changes in which new substances are formed are known as chemical changes. Some examples are burning of paper, cooking of food and rusting of iron.
- During chemical changes, the rearrangement of atoms happens to form new products.

Exercise

1 Choose the correct answer for each of the following.

a. Identify the correct balanced chemical equation from the following equations.

   i. $2BaCl_2 + Al_2(SO_4)_3 \longrightarrow 2BaSO_4 + AlCl_3$

   ii. $3BaCl_2 + 2Al_2(SO_4)_3 \longrightarrow 3BaSO_4 + AlCl_3$

   iii. $3BaCl_2 + Al_2(SO_4)_3 \longrightarrow 3BaSO_4 + 2AlCl_3$

   iv. $BaCl_2 + Al_2(SO_4)_3 \longrightarrow BaSO_4 + 2AlCl_3$

b. Chemical substances that participate in a chemical reaction are called

   i. products   ii. reactants

   iii. equations   iv. symbols

c. Which of these is a balanced chemical equation?

   i. $2Mg + 2O_2 \longrightarrow 2MgO$

   ii. $Fe + S \longrightarrow FeS$

   iii. $2H_2O \longrightarrow 2H_2 + 2O_2$

   iv. $Hg + O_2 \longrightarrow HgO$

d. Identify the product in the equation that is formed as a precipitate.

   $CuSO_4 + H_2S \longrightarrow CuS + H_2SO_4$

   i. Copper sulphate

   ii. Hydrogen sulphide

   iii. Copper sulphide

   iv. Sulphuric acid

e. When a test tube containing ammonium chloride is heated carefully over a Bunsen burner, it releases a ________.

   i. Pungent odour

   ii. Fruity odour

   iii. Flowery odour

   iv. Pleasant odour

2 Fill in the blanks.

a. The new substances formed during a chemical reaction are known as ____________ (products/reactants).

b. $CO_2 + H_2O \longrightarrow$ ____________ (H_3CO_2/H_2CO_3).

c. The reaction in which heat energy is released is known as ____________ (exothermic/endothermic) reaction.

d. A ____________ can be defined as the transformation of substance from one form to another (change/reaction).

e. Oxygen and hydrogen molecules rearrange and form water molecules with the help of ____________ bonds (physical/chemical).

3 Write T for True and F for False.

a. Some chemical reactions show a change in colour.

b. A chemical reaction expressed in words is known as a chemical equation.

c. In a chemical equation, the head of the arrow points towards the products.

d. When a chemical change takes place, new products are formed that have properties same as that of the original substance.

e. Insoluble product formed at the end of a reaction is called precipitate.

4 Complete the following chemical equations and balance them.

a. $Al +$ ____ $\longrightarrow Al_2S_3$

b. $Zn + HCl \longrightarrow$ ____ $+ H_2$

c. ____ $+ CO_2 \longrightarrow H_2CO_3$

d. $KOH +$ ____ $\longrightarrow KCl + H_2O$

e. $ZnS +$ ____ $\longrightarrow ZnO + SO_2$

f. $PbO_2 \longrightarrow$ ____ $+ O_2$

5. **Express the following word equations as balanced chemical equations.**
   a. Aluminium + Water ⟶ Aluminium oxide + Hydrogen
   b. Calcium + Oxygen ⟶ Calcium oxide
   c. Potassium chlorate ⟶ Potassium chloride + Oxygen
   d. Magnesium hydroxide ⟶ Magnesium oxide + Water

6. **Define the following terms.**
   a. Physical change
   b. Chemical change
   c. Chemical equation
   d. Reactants
   e. Products
   f. Precipitate

7. **Differentiate between the following.**
   a. Physical change and chemical change
   b. Balanced equation and unbalanced equation
   c. Displacement reaction and double displacement reaction

8. **Answer the following questions in brief.**
   a. What is a chemical reaction?
   b. What is a word equation? How is it different from a chemical equation?
   c. Why do we need to balance a chemical equation?
   d. Write balanced chemical equations for:
      i. Reaction of iron sulphide and hydrogen bromide
      ii. Decomposition of calcium carbonate
   e. Write the characteristics of chemical equations.
   f. Distinguish between exothermic and endothermic reactions.

9. **Answer the following questions in detail.**
   a. Explain the steps involved in writing a chemical equation with an example.
   b. Explain the steps involved in balancing a chemical equation with an example.
   c. What information do we get from a balanced chemical equation?
   d. Explain with an experiment formation of precipitate.
   e. Write a note on chemical equations that involves energy. Give examples for each.

10. **Think and answer.**
    a. Rohit burned a piece of coal in the presence of air. What products would you expect to be formed?
       (Hint: What is the main constituent of coal?)
    b. When calcium oxide is put into water and stirred, calcium hydroxide is formed. What kind of a reaction is it?
       (Hint: Write the skeletal equation first and then balance it.)

11. **Project**

Make a chart of chemical reactions which form coloured products. Use colour papers to represent the different compounds that take part in the reaction. Display it on your class notice board.

12. **In the Library**

Collect information on the characteristics of a chemical reaction by referring to library books.

Worksheet

Subject Integration

Perform the activity given below and answer the questions that follow.

1. Take one 250 ml glass beaker. Measure and pour 50 ml of hydrogen peroxide into the beaker.
2. Measure the temperature of hydrogen peroxide using a thermometer.
3. Add two spoons of dry yeast to the hydrogen peroxide in the beaker.
4. Using a glass rod, gently stir the contents of the solution.
5. Measure the temperature of the solution.
6. Record your observations in the table given below.

S. No	Observations	Readings
a.	Initial temperature	
b.	Final temperature	
c.	Temperature change (t) (maximum – minimum temperature)	

a. What do you conclude from the above activity?

____

____

b. Do all chemical reactions involve the absorption of heat energy from the surroundings?

____

____

c. Why is there a change of energy during chemical reactions?

____

____

Metals and Non-Metals

6

What I shall learn

- Properties of metals and non-metals
- Uses of metals and non-metals
- Rusting and various ways to prevent it
- Properties and uses of metalloids

Introduction

Different substances in our surroundings differ in their properties. Some substances are hard, while others are soft, some conduct heat and electricity, while others do not.

All elements differ from each other in their properties. However, some elements possess certain common properties as well. Based on the common properties, the elements are classified into two main groups, namely, **metals** and **non-metals**. In this chapter, we shall learn the various properties and uses of metals and non-metals.

Metals

Nearly 118 elements are known on Earth so far. Out of these, 91 elements are metals. Metals are elements that readily lose electrons to form positive ions (cations). They are mostly solid substances that are hard, opaque, lustrous, malleable, ductile, sonorous and good conductors of heat and electricity. Copper, silver, gold, sodium, iron and aluminium are a few examples of metals.

Do You Know?

Metals are also found abundantly in oceans and seas. Metals like manganese and gold are obtained from the sediments on the ocean floor. Metals like sodium, potassium, calcium and magnesium are present as dissolved salts in sea water.

Occurrence of Metals

A vast majority of metals are obtained from Earth's crust. They are found in almost all rocks and soil. Metals may occur in either free state or combined state in nature. Metals like silver, gold and platinum are non-reactive and exist in free state. Such metals are called **noble metals**. Metals like sodium, aluminium and copper are very reactive in nature and cannot exist in free state. They react with other elements and non-metals to form their respective compounds. In nature, such metals occur in the combined state in the form of **minerals**. A mineral from which a metal can be extracted in large amounts or economically is known as an **ore**.

Properties of Metals

- **Physical state**: Metals are solids at room temperature. An exception is mercury which is liquid at room temperature.
- **Lustre**: Metals are lustrous (shiny) in appearance.
- **Hardness**: All metals are hard and strong, except sodium and potassium that are soft metals and can be cut easily with a knife.
- **Malleability**: The property by which substances can be beaten into thin sheets without breaking is called malleability. Most of the metals such as copper, gold and iron are malleable in nature, whereas sodium, zinc and potassium are not.
- **Brittleness**: The property by which substances can be broken easily into pieces is called brittleness. Metals are not brittle, but sodium, potassium and zinc are brittle.
- **Ductility**: The property by which substances can be drawn into thin wires is called ductility. Metals are ductile. Exceptions are sodium, zinc and potassium.
- **Sonority**: The property by which metals can produce a ringing sound when they are struck with a hard object is called sonority. Almost all metals are sonorous.
- **Conductivity**: The property of substances to allow heat or electricity to pass through them is called conductivity. All metals are good conductors of heat and electricity.
- **Density**: Metals have high density. Thus, metals sink in water but sodium and potassium are exceptions as they float in water.
- **Melting and boiling points**: Most metals have high melting and boiling points.

Non-metals

Of the 118 known elements on Earth, 17 are non-metals. Non-metals are elements that readily accept electrons to form negative ions (anions). They are either solid or gaseous substances that are soft, lack lustre, non-malleable, non-ductile, non-sonorous and poor conductors of heat and electricity. Carbon, sulphur, hydrogen, oxygen and nitrogen are a few examples of non-metals.

Occurrence of Non-metals

Non-metals are found in Earth's atmosphere, crust and sometimes even in oceans. In nature, non-metals may occur either in free state or in combined state. Some non-metals can occur in both free and combined states. For example, in the free state, oxygen occurs in the atmosphere, while in the combined state, oxygen occurs in the crust as oxides of compounds. Non-metals like helium, neon, argon, krypton, xenon and radon occur only in the free state in nature and are called noble gases.

Properties of Non-metals

- **Physical state**: Non-metals are solids or gases at room temperature. An exception is bromine, which exists in the liquid state at room temperature.
- **Lustre**: Non-metals are generally non-lustrous in appearance. Exceptions are graphite and iodine, which have lustre.
- **Hardness**: Most non-metals are soft. Diamond is an exception, which is hard.

- **Malleability**: Most of the non-metals are non-malleable in nature.
- **Brittleness**: Most of the non-metals are brittle.
- **Ductility**: Non-metals cannot be drawn into wires, that is, they are non-ductile.
- **Sonority**: All non-metals are non-sonorous.
- **Conductivity**: Most non-metals are poor conductors of heat and electricity. An exception is graphite, which is a good conductor of heat and electricity.
- **Density**: Non-metals have low density.
- **Melting and boiling points**: Non-metals have low melting and boiling points. Graphite is an exception.

Table 6.1 Comparison of properties of metals and non-metals

Metals	Non-metals
Metals are usually solids at room temperature and crystalline in nature.	Non-metals mostly exist in solid or gaseous state at room temperature.
Metals have a shiny surface.	Non-metals are not shiny in appearance.
Metals are hard.	Non-metals are soft.
Most of the metals are malleable.	Non-metals are not malleable.
Metals are not brittle.	Non-metals are brittle.
Generally, most metals are ductile.	Generally, non-metals are non-ductile.
Generally, metals are good conductors of heat and electricity.	Generally, non-metals are bad conductors of heat and electricity.
Metals are sonorous.	Non-metals are non-sonorous.
Metals have high density.	Non-metals have low density.

Rusting

It is the process of formation of a reddish-brown, flaky substance on the surface of iron objects in the presence of moisture (water vapour) and air (oxygen). This reddish-brown deposit formed on iron objects is known as **rust**.

The presence of both water vapour and oxygen is necessary for the process of rusting to occur.

$$4Fe + 3O_2 + nH_2O \longrightarrow 2Fe_2O_3.nH_2O$$

Iron + Oxygen + Moisture → Hydrated iron or ferric oxide (rust)

▲ Rust formed on an iron ship

▲ Rusting of iron

Challenge Yourself

Place an iron nail near the kitchen sink and another in the balcony. Which nail will rust faster? Why?

Science in Context

Corrosion is the process in which the surface of metals is slowly eaten away due to chemical reactions between the metal, and atmospheric oxygen and moisture. When the metal is iron, it is called rusting.

▲ Corrosion of copper

Corrosion of copper: Copper reacts with carbon dioxide in the presence of moisture to form a green substance, which is a mixture of copper hydroxide and copper carbonate.

Corrosion of silver: Silver reacts with hydrogen sulphide gas present in the atmosphere to form a black layer of silver sulphide.

▲ Corrosion of silver

Rusting is a slow and undesirable chemical change that takes place over a period of time. It weakens the strength of iron objects, thus making them brittle. Even big objects like ships and bridges are built of iron and damage to such objects leads to a big loss. Hence, rusting should be prevented to avoid the loss of iron objects.

Methods to Prevent Rusting

Rusting can be prevented by blocking the contact of iron objects with moisture and air. The following methods can be used to prevent rusting.

- **Painting**: Applying a coat of paint on iron objects prevents rusting. The layer of paint prevents the contact of air or moisture with iron.
- **Oiling or greasing**: A thin layer of oil or grease is applied on the surface of iron objects like tools and machines. This prevents the contact of air or moisture with tools and machines.

▲ Enameled vessel

- **Galvanizing**: The process of coating iron objects with a thin layer of zinc metal is known as **galvanization**. Zinc is a corrosion-resistant metal. For example, iron pipes used for supplying water to our homes are galvanized to prevent rusting.
- **Electroplating**: The process of coating iron objects with a thin layer of metals that do not corrode is called **electroplating**. Metals such as nickel, chromium, copper, silver or gold are used as they are less reactive with oxygen. For example, kitchen articles like spoons and forks are coated with silver, and taps and wheel rims are coated with chromium to prevent rusting and also to improve their appearance.
- **Coating with enamel**: Objects like cooking vessels, refrigerators and stoves are coated with a layer of enamel to protect them from rusting.
- **Tin plating**: Tin is non-toxic, corrosion-resistant and less reactive than iron. Some iron objects are coated with a thin layer of tin to prevent them from rusting. Food packaging cans are coated with tin.
- **Alloying**: Iron is mixed with metals like nickel and chromium, which are corrosion-resistant, to form alloys. Stainless steel is one such alloy. It is resistant to rust. Hence, it is used to make cooking utensils.

Do You Know?

The iron pillar in Delhi near Qutub Minar, built about 1600 years ago, has not rusted even till today. The monument has attracted many scientists and metallurgists from all over the world due to its unique feature.

Activity 1

Aim: To prove that rusting occurs in the presence of both air and moisture

Materials required: Three iron nails, three glass test tubes with cork, quick lime (calcium oxide), measuring cylinder, water, test tube stand and dilute acid (HCl or H_2SO_4)

Procedure:

1. Take the three glass test tubes and put one iron nail in each of them.
2. Pour tap water (10 ml) in the first test tube.
3. Add some quick lime (calcium oxide) in the second test tube.
4. Pour tap water (10 ml) in the third test tube and add few drops of dilute acid (HCl or H_2SO_4).
5. The nail should be completely immersed in water.
6. Seal the mouth of all the three test tubes with rubber corks and keep them in a test tube stand.

Observation:

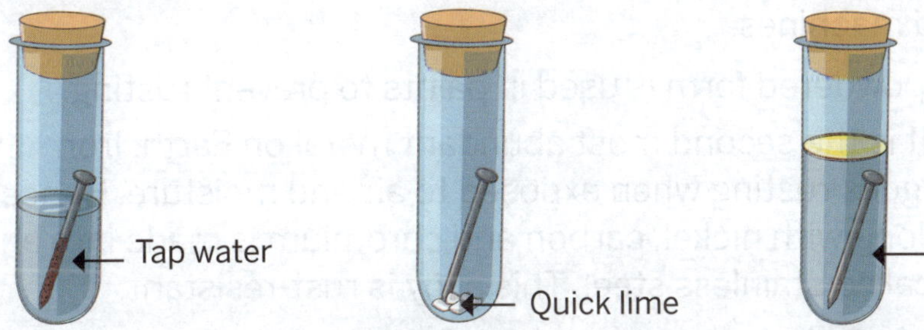

S.No.	Experimental Set-Up	Observation	Inference
1	Set-up 1 (water + iron nail)	Iron nail rusts.	Rusting occurs due to the availability of both air and moisture.
2	Set-up 2 (calcium oxide + iron nail)	Iron nail does not rust.	Rusting does not occur as calcium oxide (quick lime) absorbs the moisture that is available in the test tube and also there is no availability of air.
3	Set-up 3 (water + dilute acid (HCl or H_2SO_4))	Iron nail reacts with the dilute acid.	Due to the reaction of dilute acid and iron nail, the iron nail may get dissolved in the dilute acid gradually.

Conclusion: This proves that both air (oxygen) and moisture are required for rusting.

Revision Zone

Write T for True and F for False.

1. Silver, gold and platinum metals exist in free state and are non-reactive.
2. Rusting occurs in the presence of both air and moisture.
3. This reddish-brown deposit formed on iron objects is known as rust.
4. Most of the non-metals are malleable.
5. Metals are non-sonorous.

▲ Aluminium can

Science in Context

Aluminium does not react with air because as soon as it is exposed to air, it reacts and forms a layer of oxide (aluminium oxide) on its surface and this prevents further reaction from taking place. Hence, it does not rust.

Uses of Metals

Metals are widely used in our daily lives for various purposes. Depending upon their properties, metals are used for specific purposes. Uses of some common metals are given below.

Aluminium: It is the most abundant metal on Earth. Aluminium is a lightweight and strong metal. It is a good conductor of heat and electricity.

- It is used for making high-voltage electrical cables and wires.
- It is used for making furniture, doors and windows, cooking utensils, and construction materials.
- Aluminium foil is used for the packaging of food materials and medicines.
- It is used in making body parts of aircraft, vehicles and machines.
- Its powdered form is used in paints to prevent rusting.

Iron: It is the second most abundant metal on Earth. Iron undergoes rusting when exposed to air and moisture. Hence, iron along with nickel, carbon and chromium is made into an alloy called stainless steel. This alloy is rust-resistant.

- It is used to make water pipes, furniture, surgical instruments, railings, nuts, bolts, tools, warships and tanks.
- It is used for making bridges, parts of vehicles, machines and utensils. It is also widely used in the construction industry.
- It is used in the preparation of ammonia gas.

▲ Iron pipes

▲ Iron bolts

Copper: It is the best conductor of heat and electricity after silver.

- It is used in making electrical wires and cables.
- It is used for making circuits in electrical appliances like televisions and computers.
- It is used for making jewellery and coins.
- It is used for manufacturing boiler pipes, car radiators and cooking utensils.

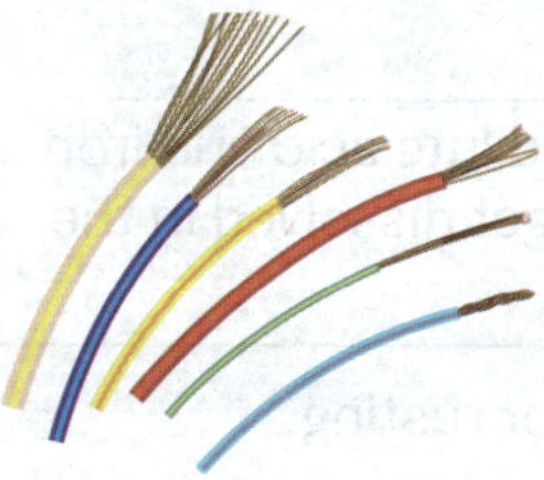

▲ Electrical wires

Gold: It is a precious and an expensive metal. Gold does not react with moisture (water) and atmospheric oxygen (air), and hence, it does not get tarnished.

- It is used for making coins, ornaments and jewellery.
- It is also used for coating artificial jewellery.
- It is used to fill tooth cavities and make tooth caps.

▲ Gold coins

Silver: It is the best conductor of heat and electricity. Silver reacts with sulphur compounds present in the air and gets tarnished.

- It is used in making jewellery, coins and decorative articles.
- It is used to fill cavities and make tooth caps.
- It is used for making circuits in sensitive electronic devices.
- Salts of silver are used in making photographic films.
- It is used in making mirrors and for electroplating.

▲ Silver spoons

Magnesium: It is a light metal that burns with a white-coloured flame.

- As it is a flammable metal, it is used in fireworks to give a sparkling effect.
- It is used in making fuse wires in electronic devices.
- Compounds of magnesium are used in medicines.

▲ Galvanized tub

Zinc: It is resistant to rusting. Hence, zinc is used to protect iron from rusting.

- It is used for making galvanized iron pipes as it protects iron from corrosion. Iron objects are coated with a thin layer of zinc and this process is called **galvanization**.
- It is used in dry cells.

Science in Context

Mercury is used in thermometers because it expands easily when the temperature increases.

Mercury: It is a silvery metal and a good conductor of heat.

- It is used in thermometers. Its lustrous nature helps in reading the temperature easily.
- It is used in barometers and other laboratory equipment.
- It is used in the field of dentistry to make fillings for tooth cavities.

Lead: It is a highly malleable and ductile metal. It is a poor conductor of electricity.

- It is used in making flexible water pipes, X-ray shields and storage batteries.
- It is used as a covering for electrical wires and cables.

▲ Tin can

Tin: It is resistant to rusting and does not react with acids present in food items.

- Objects made of iron are coated with a thin layer of tin. This protects iron objects from rusting. Food cans or containers are often plated with tin.
- It is used to make alloys like bronze and solder.

Uses of Non-metals

Carbon: It is one of the most essential elements in nature. It can occur in both free and combined states in nature.

Do You Know?

Carbon (along with hydrogen and oxygen) is present as the central element in carbohydrates, proteins and fats. These molecules form the structural and functional components of all living cells.

▲ Diamond jewellery

▲ Pencil lead

Carbon in combination with hydrogen forms a set of important compounds called **hydrocarbons**. They are mainly found in fuels like biogas, petrol, diesel and LPG. Apart from these, carbon is also found in the form of graphite, diamond and charcoal.

- Diamond is the hardest substance known on Earth. Hence, it is used to cut glass, hard metals and rocks. It is also used for making jewellery.
- Graphite is used to manufacture the lead of pencils.
- It is used as electrodes in cells and batteries.
- Graphite is used as a lubricant in machine parts.
- Coal, which is also a form of carbon, is widely used as a fuel in industries and homes.
- Charcoal is used as a fuel. It is used to make gunpowder and in water filters for removing impurities.

Hydrogen: It is a colourless, odourless and inflammable gas. Hydrogen is the lightest element. It is found in the combined state in water, acids and other chemical compounds.

- Hydrogen is used in the manufacturing of *vanaspati (ghee)* from vegetable oil. This process is called **hydrogenation of vegetable oil**.
- It is used in the manufacturing of ammonia gas and methanol.
- It is used as a rocket fuel.

Oxygen: It is the most abundant element in Earth's crust. It is a colourless, tasteless and odourless gas. About 21 per cent of the air (by volume) is composed of oxygen.

- It is required for combustion of fuels. Without oxygen, combustion of a fuel cannot occur.
- It is essential for respiration in living organisms.
- Oxygen cylinders are used in hospitals and by deep-sea divers and mountaineers for oxygen supply or breathing.
- It is used in welding in combination with other gases.

Nitrogen: It is a colourless, tasteless and odourless gas. Nitrogen is the most abundant gas in the atmosphere (about 78 per cent by volume). It is the basic element of all plant and animal proteins.

- It is used in food packaging as it removes the oxygen and moisture content, and thus prevents spoilage of food.
- It is used in the preparation of nitric acid, ammonia and nitrogen fertilizers.
- In liquid form, nitrogen is used as a cooling agent in refrigerators.

Chlorine: It is a very reactive non-metal and does not occur in free state. It is found in sea water and salt beds in the form of salts like sodium chloride, calcium chloride, magnesium chloride and potassium chloride.

- It is used as a disinfectant to sterilize drinking water and water in swimming pools. Addition of chlorine tablets in water to kill germs is called **chlorination**.
- It is used in making bleaching powder, pesticides and insecticides.
- It is used in making laboratory chemicals like hydrochloric acid.

Iodine: It is a rare element and exists mainly in ocean water. It is required for the proper functioning of the thyroid gland in human beings.

- It is used in the preparation of tincture of iodine which is used as an antiseptic and a disinfectant.
- It is used to make iodized salt by adding sodium or potassium iodide to common salt.
- It is used to prepare photographic films.

Phosphorus: It is an extremely reactive element. It may exist as red or white phosphorus.

- It is used in the manufacturing of matchsticks, fertilizers, fireworks, smokescreens, phosphoric acid and superphosphate (a fertilizer).
- It is used in making baking powder and light emitting diodes (LEDs).

Sulphur: It is a yellow, crystalline solid that is insoluble in water.

- It is used in agriculture as insecticides and fungicides.
- It is used in making skin ointments and medical creams.
- It is used in the preparation of sulphuric acid, gunpowder, plastics, detergents, synthetic fibres and explosives.

Helium: It is a noble gas. It is the second lightest element. Helium is lighter than air.

- It is used for filling hot-air balloons for flying and weather balloons for studying the weather.
- It is mixed with oxygen in cylinders carried by deep-sea divers.
- It is used for welding.

Argon: It is a noble gas.

- It is filled in electric bulbs and tube lights. This gives an inert atmosphere to the filament of the bulb.
- It is used for welding and in glow signboards.

Neon: It is also a noble gas.

- It is used in fluorescent bulbs, which are used in advertising boards and billboards.
- It is used in television tubes, indicator lights and brake lights.

Science in Context

Chlorine, bromine, iodine and fluorine belong to a group of elements called **halogens**. These non-metals are very reactive and do not exist in free state in nature.

Do You Know?

Deficiency of iodine in the human body leads to a disease called goitre. Goitre results in enlargement of the thyroid gland.

Science in Context

Phosphorus can catch fire when exposed to air. So, it is usually stored in water as it does not react with water.

▲ Helium balloons

Metalloids

Some elements exhibit the properties of both metals as well as non-metals. Such elements are known as **metalloids**.

Characteristics of Metalloids

- Metalloids have metallic appearance.
- They are brittle.
- They are fair conductors of electricity.
- They combine with metals and result in the formation of alloys.
- They are positioned in the periodic table on either side of the metals and non-metals.

Table 6.2 Properties and uses of few metalloids

Element	Properties	Uses
Silicon 	• It is a crystalline solid and has blue-grey metallic lustre. • It can dissolve in hot aqueous alkalis and liberate hydrogen gas similar to the metals like aluminium and zinc. • It is covalent in nature like non-metals. • It can form alloys by reacting with metals like copper and iron. • It reacts with oxygen to form silicones. These silicones are resistant to heat and moisture.	• It is used in the manufacturing of integrated microchips and semiconductors. • Silica (sand) is used in the manufacturing of cement, glass and porcelain. • It is used as an insulating material in electrical appliances.
Germanium 	• It is a metalloid with gray-white appearance, hard, lustrous and brittle in nature. • It is a semiconductor. • The liquid germanium acts as a metallic conductor that has electrical conductivity similar to liquid mercury. • It can form alloys by reacting with the metals like gold and aluminium. • Like metals they form the less stable divalent compounds and tetravalent compounds. • Due to the solubility of germanium monoxide in acidic solutions, it is mostly considered as a metal.	• It is used in electronic applications as a transistor. • It is used as objective lenses for microscopes and in camera lenses. • It is used as a catalyst. • It is extensively used in the infrared spectroscopes.

Element	Properties	Uses
Tungsten 	• It has high ductility and melting point. • It has lowest vapor pressure. • It has the high tensile strength and has corrosion-resistant property. • It is used in the formation of alloys like steel.	• It is used in the fluorescent light bulb filaments and incandescent lights. • It is also used in the X-ray production. • It is used in the television tubes as the primary element.
Antimony 	• It is hard, silvery and brittle with lustre. • It can form alloys by reacting with the metals like nickel, copper, zinc and aluminium. This alloy can expand on cooling. • It is a weak conductor of heat and electricity.	• It is used in the making of semiconductor devices like diodes and infrared detectors. • It is also used in the synthesis of materials like glass, bullets, batteries, paints and enamels and as a flame retardant.

Revision Zone

Write T for True and F for False.

1. Zinc is used in the manufacturing of fireworks.
2. All non-metals are malleable and ductile.
3. Sulphur is used in the preparation of gunpowder.
4. Helium is used for filling hot-air balloons because it is lighter than air.
5. Metalloids have metallic appearance.

Keywords

Ore: a mineral from which a metal can be extracted in large amounts

Malleability: the property of substances that can be beaten into thin sheets without breaking

Ductility: the property of substances that can be drawn into thin wires

Conductivity: the property of substances to allow heat or electricity to pass through them

Corrosion: the process in which atmospheric moisture and gases slowly eat away the surface of metals

Rusting: the process of formation of a reddish-brown, flaky substance on the surface of iron objects in the presence of moisture and oxygen

Galvanization: the process of coating iron objects with a thin layer of zinc metal

Electroplating: the process of coating iron objects with a thin layer of metals that do not corrode

Hydrogenation: the process of manufacturing of vanaspati (ghee) from vegetable oil

Metalloids: the elements that exhibit the properties of both metals as well as non-metals

In a Nutshell

- Metals are mostly solid substances that are hard, lustrous, malleable, ductile, sonorous and good conductors of heat and electricity.
- Non-metals are substances that are usually soft, lack lustre, non-malleable, non-ductile and non-sonorous and are poor conductors of heat and electricity.
- Rusting is the process of formation of a reddish-brown, flaky substance on the surface of iron objects in the presence of moisture (water vapour) and air (oxygen).
- Rusting can be prevented by blocking the contact of iron objects with moisture and air by the following methods like painting, oiling or greasing, galvanizing, electroplating and alloying.
- Metalloids are the elements that exhibit the properties of both metals as well as non-metals.

Exercise

1 Choose the correct answer for each of the following.

a. Which of the following metal is not ductile in nature?
   i. Copper
   ii. Aluminium
   iii. Silver
   iv. Potassium

b. Which of these non-metals is a good conductor of electricity?
   i. Iodine
   ii. Nitrogen
   iii. Diamond
   iv. Graphite

c. The metal that is very soft and can be cut with a knife is
   i. Potassium
   ii. Iron
   iii. Sodium
   iv. Carbon

d. The non-metal that is a good conductor of electricity is
   i. Chlorine
   ii. Nitrogen
   iii. Graphite
   iv. Oxygen

e. Which of these following is malleable in nature?
   i. Coal
   ii. Graphite
   iii. Copper
   iv. Diamond

2 Fill in the blanks.

a. The property by which substances can be drawn into thin wires is known as ________ (ductility/malleability).

b. The property by which metals can be beaten into thin sheets is called ________ (sonority/malleability).

c. ________ (Lead/Zinc) is used in the galvanization of iron pipes.

d. ________ (Oxygen/Nitrogen) is used in food packaging to prevent spoilage of food.

e. Sulphur is used to make ________ (skin ointments/baking powder).

3 Write T for True and F for False.

a. Materials other than metals are not sonorous.

b. Metals are good conductors of electricity.

c. Sulphur is malleable.

d. Iodine is a non-metal that has a shiny experience.

e. Lead is used in making X-ray shields.

4 Define the following terms.

a. Alloying

b. Metalloids

c. Hydrocarbons

d. Chlorination

e. Hydrogenation

5 Differentiate between the following.

a. Metalloids and metals

b. Minerals and ores

c. Metals and non-metals

d. Painting and greasing

e. Electroplating and galvanization

6 Give reasons for the following.

a. Magnesium is used in manufacturing of fireworks.

b. The preference of gold in making jewellery.
c. Chlorine is used to sterilize water.
d. Coating of wheel rims and taps with chromium.
e. Stainless steel is used in the making of cooking utensils.

7 Answer the following questions in brief.

a. What is rust? Give its chemical formula.
b. How ductility is different from sonority?
c. Write any two properties of metals?
d. Mention any two properties of non-metals.
e. What are the conditions essential for the process of rusting?

8 Answer the following questions in detail.

a. Compare the general properties of metals and non-metals.
b. List the uses of any four metals.
c. Mention the uses of any four non-metals.
d. Describe the properties and uses of any two metalloids.
e. Explain the different methods used for prevention of rusting.

9 Think and answer.

The black material present in the pencil is a metal or a non-metal? (Hint: Recollect the properties of non-metals)

10 Project

Make a scrapbook by collecting pictures of various objects made of different metals and non-metals. For images of objects, use pictures from magazines, newspapers and books

11 In the Library

Collect information about 'electroplating technique' and its importance in the prevention of corrosion.

Worksheet

Subject Integration

Look at the two electrical circuits given below and answer the questions that follow.

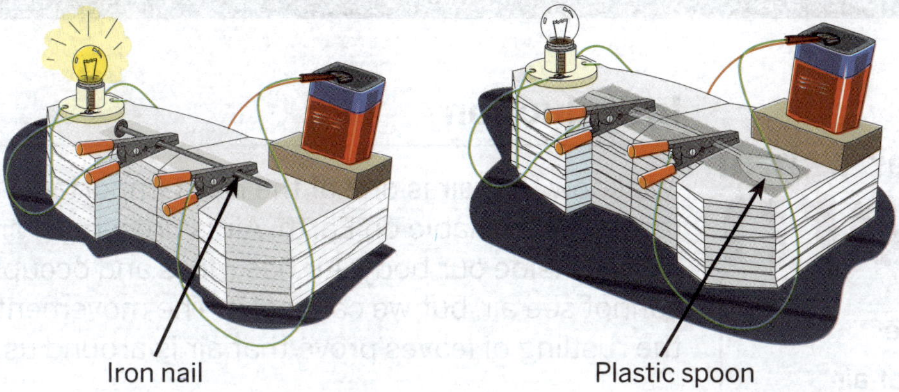

a. Which of the two given materials is a conductor of electricity and which one is an insulator?

b. Why is the conductor able to conduct electricity? Give reasons.

c. The same activity is done by using the materials listed in the table given below. Identify and write whether these materials are conductors or insulators.

Material	Conductor/Insulator
Copper rod	
Steel spoon	
Plastic comb	
Wooden picce	
Metallic paper clip	
Aluminium wire	

Air and Atmosphere

7

What I shall learn

- Air is a mixture
- Composition of air
- Combustion
- Acid rain
- Air quality
- Properties of oxygen

Introduction

We know that air is one of the most important natural resources available on Earth. Air is present all around us as well as inside our body. Air has mass and occupies space. We cannot see air, but we can feel it. The movement of a kite and the rustling of leaves prove that air is around us.

A thick blanket of air called the **atmosphere** envelopes Earth and protects it from harmful ultraviolet radiations of the Sun. It also helps in maintaining a proper temperature on Earth, which enables the survival of all living things. We learned in class 6 that air is a mixture of gases like oxygen, carbon dioxide and nitrogen. These gases are present in uniform composition and thus, air is a homogeneous mixture.

Composition of Air

The main constituents of air are nitrogen (around 78 per cent), oxygen (around 21 per cent), carbon dioxide (around 0.03 per cent) and inert gases (around 0.9 per cent). Apart from these gases, small quantities of water vapour, dust, smoke and few pollutants are also present in the air. The amount of these constituents varies in different regions from time to time. Table 7.1 gives the volume (in percentage) of the constituents of air.

Table 7.1 Constituents of air and their percentages

Constituent of air	Percentage by volume
Nitrogen	78%
Oxygen	21%
Carbon dioxide	0.03%
Inert gases	0.9%
Water vapour	Varies
Others like dust and smoke	Varies

Each constituent of air retains its properties. It does not react with other constituents. The composition of air varies from place to place and from season to season. For example, the amount of water vapour in the air is more in coastal regions than in deserts. Cities have a high amount of pollutants due to increased dust and smoke released from vehicles, factories, etc.

Nitrogen

Nitrogen is the most abundant gas in the atmosphere. It is colourless and odourless. It is required to form the basic building block of all proteins in living organisms. Therefore, nitrogen is required for the growth and development of all living organisms. Some bacteria present in the soil convert atmospheric nitrogen into compounds which can be taken up and used by plants. Animals obtain nitrogen from plant and animal sources of food.

Oxygen

Oxygen is the second most abundant gas in the atmosphere. It is a chemically reactive gas. All living organisms such as fish, animals, insects, birds and human beings breathe in oxygen. Thus, oxygen is required by all living things to survive.

Oxygen is used to obtain energy from the food we eat. This process is called respiration. Oxygen supports combustion and is thus required to burn fuels. Plants constantly replenish oxygen in the atmosphere during the process of photosynthesis.

Carbon Dioxide

Air contains around 0.03 per cent of carbon dioxide. Carbon dioxide is also a chemically reactive gas. It plays an important role as green plants prepare their food using carbon dioxide from air during photosynthesis. Carbon dioxide does not support combustion. Carbon dioxide is released by living things during respiration. It is also released during combustion of substances. A slight increase in the percentage of carbon dioxide increases the overall temperature of Earth. This condition is known as **global warming**.

Inert Gases

Inert gases are a group of gases that are non-reactive and stable. These are also called noble gases. They are present in traces in air. These gases can be isolated from air. Argon, neon, helium, krypton, xenon and radon are common inert gases present in air. Argon, krypton, neon and xenon are mostly used for lighting purposes like in advertising sign boards, light bulbs and lamps. Helium is used in hot-air balloons. Radon is used in the treatment of cancer.

Water Vapour

The amount of water vapour present in the air in a particular place is known as atmospheric humidity. Evaporation from water bodies and transpiration from plants are the two sources of water vapour. Water vapour keeps the air cool and is also a part of the water cycle. So, it helps in the formation of clouds and acts as an important source of water for all living things on Earth. As a result, water vapour is also responsible for climatic changes.

Combustion

The process of burning of substances in the presence of oxygen to release heat and light energy is called **combustion**. In other words, a chemical reaction in which a substance reacts rapidly with oxygen to produce new substances and to release heat and light energy is called combustion. Any substance that undergoes combustion is called a **fuel**. A fuel undergoes combustion only when it has attained (or is heated

▲ Burning of fuels requires oxygen

to) a certain minimum temperature. The minimum temperature at which a substance starts burning is called its **ignition temperature**.

$$\text{Fuels + Oxygen} \xrightarrow{\text{heat}} \text{Carbon dioxide + Water vapour + Energy}$$

The energy produced during combustion is used in cooking, to run automobiles, in industries to produce energy and for various other purposes. Commonly used fuels are coal, wood, petrol, diesel, kerosene, CNG and LPG.

During combustion of these fuels, carbon dioxide and water are released. Some combustion reactions are as follows:

- Hydrogen is used as a rocket fuel. It burns in the presence of oxygen to form water.

$$2H_2 + O_2 \longrightarrow 2H_2O$$

- Coal is used as a fuel in thermal power stations. It mainly consists of carbon, which burns to form carbon dioxide.

$$C + O_2 \longrightarrow CO_2$$

- Petrol, diesel and kerosene are mainly made of carbon and hydrogen, while biogas and CNG are made of methane. When these fuels burn, they form carbon dioxide and water.

$$CH_4 + 2O_2 \longrightarrow CO_2 + 2H_2O$$

Activity 1

Aim: To show that oxygen is necessary for burning

Materials required: Two candles, jar or glass and matchstick

Procedure:

1. Place the two candles on a table and light them.
2. After a while, invert the jar or glass over one of the candles.

Observation: The candle which is exposed to air continues to burn, whereas the candle covered by the glass burns for a short while and then stops burning.

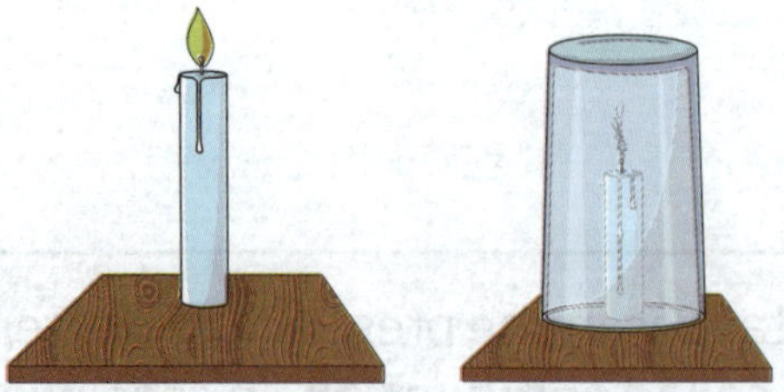

Conclusion: When the oxygen available inside the inverted glass is completely used up for burning, the candle stops burning. This proves that oxygen is necessary for burning.

Mass Change During Burning

Burning of magnesium: During combustion or burning, there is a change in the mass of products formed. Let us learn about it by doing the following activity.

Activity 2

To be demonstrated by the teacher

Aim: To observe the mass change during the burning of magnesium in the presence of atmospheric oxygen.

Materials required: Magnesium ribbon, Bunsen burner, weighing balance, crucible with lid, tripod stand, pipe-clay triangle, lighter or matchstick, a pair of tongs

Procedure:

- Take a clean piece of magnesium ribbon (8–10 cm long).
- With the help of weighing balance measure the weight of the crucible with the lid and note it as 'mass 1'.
- Now place the magnesium ribbon into the crucible and measure the weight of the crucible containing magnesium with the lid and note it as 'mass 2'.
- Set up the Bunsen burner and place a tripod stand. Now place the crucible on a tripod stand over pipe-clay triangle.
- Now light the Bunsen burner with the help of a lighter or matchstick and heat the crucible.
- Once the heating process is on, gently try to lift the lid of the crucible with the tongs in order to allow the oxygen to pass into the crucible.
- Continue the above process until you see no further reaction.
- Now turn off the Bunsen burner and let the apparatus cool.
- Reweigh the contents of crucible with the lid and note it as 'mass 3'.

Conclusion: We can clearly observe the increase in weight (mass 3) after the chemical reaction. This increase in mass is due to the formation of a new product (magnesium oxide) as magnesium gains oxygen from the atmosphere.

In the above activity, magnesium reacts with the atmospheric oxygen to form magnesium oxide. The word equation of the chemical reaction would be:

$$\text{Magnesium} + \text{Oxygen} \longrightarrow \text{Magnesium oxide}$$

The chemical equation of this chemical reaction would be:

$$Mg + O_2 \longrightarrow MgO$$

The number of atoms of each element on both the sides should be equal (as per the law of conservation of mass, which states that mass is neither created nor destroyed), that is, the equation should be balanced.

$$\text{Magnesium (2Mg)} + \text{Oxygen } (O_2) \longrightarrow \text{Magnesium oxide (2MgO)}$$

(Reactants) (Product)

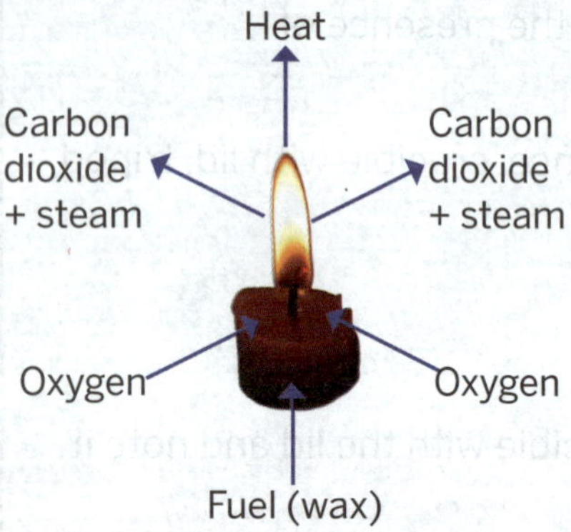

Burning of Candle: The candle wax is a composition of organic compound. During the burning process some of the wax particles get vaporized resulting in the formation of carbon dioxide, water and other organic products. The mass of the candle decreases as these wax particles will be lost during the burning process.

Note: Theoretically, as per **the law of conservation of mass**, mass is neither created nor destroyed. This is difficult to prove experimentally as during the burning process of candle, few of the products get vaporized.

Reactions of Metals and Non-metals With Oxygen

Metals and non-metals react with oxygen to form metal oxides and non-metallic oxides respectively. Some of the word equations of reactions are as follows.

Metals

- Magnesium, on heating, burns with a dazzling white flame in the presence of oxygen to form magnesium oxide.

$$\text{Magnesium} + \text{Oxygen} \xrightarrow{\text{Heat}} \text{Magnesium oxide}$$

- Sodium reacts vigorously with oxygen at room temperature to form sodium oxide.

$$\text{Sodium} + \text{Oxygen} \longrightarrow \text{Sodium oxide}$$

- Like sodium, potassium also reacts vigorously with oxygen at room temperature to form potassium oxide.

$$\text{Potassium} + \text{Oxygen} \longrightarrow \text{Potassium oxide}$$

- When calcium is heated in the presence of oxygen, it reacts to form calcium oxide.

$$\text{Calcium} + \text{Oxygen} \xrightarrow{\text{Heat}} \text{Calcium oxide}$$

Non-metals

- Sulphur burns in the presence of oxygen to form sulphur dioxide.

$$\text{Sulphur} + \text{Oxygen} \xrightarrow{\text{Heat}} \text{Sulphur dioxide}$$

- Carbon burns in the presence of oxygen to form carbon dioxide.

$$\text{Carbon} + \text{Oxygen} \xrightarrow{\text{Heat}} \text{Carbon dioxide}$$

- Phosphorous reacts with oxygen to form phosphorus pentaoxide.

$$\text{Phosphorus} + \text{Oxygen} \longrightarrow \text{Phosphorus pentaoxide}$$

Revision Zone

Fill in the blanks.

1. The chemical substances that participate in a chemical reaction are known as __________ (products/reactants)
2. Combustion of petrol releases __________ and water. (nitrogen/carbondioxide)
3. Global warming is caused by __________ gas. (carbon dioxide/oxygen)
4. The percent of __________ gas is 21% in atmosphere. (nitrogen/oxygen)

Acid Rain

Oxides of sulphur and nitrogen are the main pollutants that cause acid rain. Sulphur dioxide is mainly released during the burning of coal in thermal power stations. Nitrogen dioxide is mostly released by vehicles that run on petrol and diesel. These pollutants react with water vapour in air to form acids like sulphuric acid and nitric acid in the atmosphere. These acids mix with rain to form acid rain. Acid rain changes the composition of soil and pollutes water bodies, thus adversely affecting plant and aquatic life. It occurs more frequently in cities where pollution levels are high. It corrodes buildings (limestone and marble structures) and statues. These air pollutants can cause irritation in eyes, nose and throat, respiratory diseases, cancer and skin disorders.

How Is Acid Rain Formed?

- The pollutants like (sulphur dioxide and nitrogen dioxide) are released from the automobiles and industries.
- These pollutants react with the water vapour in the atmosphere to form strong acids like sulphuric acid and nitric acid. So, the rain water becomes acidic.

$SO_2 + H_2O \longrightarrow H_2SO_3$ (Sulphurous acid)

$SO_2 + O_3$ (Ozone) $\longrightarrow SO_3 + O_2$

$SO_3 + H_2O \longrightarrow H_2SO_4$ (Sulphuric acid)

$2NO + O_2 \longrightarrow 2NO_2$

$2NO_2 + H_2O \longrightarrow HNO_3$ (Nitric acid) + HNO_2 (Nitrous acid)

- These acids may deposit in the form of wet deposits and fall on the Earth as 'acid rain'.

Effects of Acid Rain

- Corrodes buildings and historic monuments made of limestone, marbles and metals
- Causes irritation of eyes and the skin of human beings
- Reduces soil fertility as it increases acidity of the soil
- Acidification of soil damages crops and forests due to poor availability of water and loss of nutrients
- Decolourizes the leaf pigments and causes chlorosis
- Leads to the death of aquatic organisms as it causes acidification of lakes, ponds and streams

Effect of acid rain on Taj Mahal: Taj Mahal situated in Agra is affected due to acid rain. Due to corrosion by acid rain, the marbles have lost their lustre. Acid rain reacts with the calcium carbonate (marble) of Taj Mahal and results in the colour change of the marble to light yellow.

Air Quality

Due to increase in population, rapid industrialization and human activities like burning of fuels in vehicles and cutting down of trees, the quality of air is declining. Harmful and undesirable substances get added to the air leading to air pollution. The introduction of harmful and undesirable substances in large amounts into the air as a result of human activities or natural processes, such that it affects the health of all living things, is called air pollution. Such harmful and undesirable substances are called pollutants. Let us learn about the common pollutants and their effects.

▲ Smoke from factories causes air pollution

- **Carbon monoxide (CO)**: It is produced mainly due to incomplete combustion of fuels. The sources of carbon monoxide are burning of wood and oil at homes and in factories. Petrol and diesel combustion in automobiles also releases carbon monoxide into the atmosphere. Carbon monoxide, when inhaled, mixes with the blood and prevents it from carrying oxygen in the body, thus leading to carbon monoxide poisoning. This causes headache, dizziness, suffocation and even death.
- **Carbon dioxide (CO_2)**: It is produced due to the burning of fuels. Plants use carbon dioxide during photosynthesis. However, due to deforestation, the level of carbon dioxide in the atmosphere has increased considerably, thus causing adverse effects on both plants and animals. Carbon dioxide is a greenhouse gas and the main cause of global warming.

Do You Know?

Smog is formed by the combination of smoke and fog. Smog causes respiratory disorders like bronchitis and asthma. It also reduces visibility resulting in road accidents.

- **Suspended particulate matter (SPM)**: The minute particles of soot (fine particles of unburnt carbon) and dust suspended in air form suspended particulate matters (SPMs). Soot comes from the smoke released by vehicles, chimneys of factories and burning of fuels. Dust is produced by moving vehicles and construction activities. SPMs cannot be filtered by the hair in our nostrils. So, they are a major cause of lung diseases like asthma and bronchitis, irritation in eyes and decreased vision. Burning of fuels can also release heavy metals like lead and cadmium into the air, which damage the nervous system, kidney, etc. Deposition of SPMs on plant leaves disturbs the process of photosynthesis.
- **Chlorofluorocarbons (CFCs)**: These are chemical substances that are used in refrigerators, air conditioning systems and aerosol cans. CFCs reach the atmosphere and deplete the ozone layer leading to thinning of the ozone layer or decrease in the ozone concentration in Earth's atmosphere. Due to this, a huge hole has formed in this layer called the **ozone hole**. Harmful UV rays of the sun enter Earth's atmosphere and reach its surface through this hole. UV rays can cause damage to the eyes and skin, and lead to sunburn and skin cancer.

Challenge Yourself

You, as an individual, can also help to prevent or reduce air pollution. How? Discuss ways to prevent pollution with your classmates.

Properties of Oxygen

Physical Properties

- Oxygen is a colourless, tasteless and odourless gas.
- Oxygen supports combustion, but it is itself a noncombustible gas.
- It is slightly soluble in water and slightly denser than air.
- Under very high pressure and low temperature, oxygen can be liquefied.

Know the Scientist

Carl Wilhelm Scheele (1742–1786) was a Swedish pharmacist. He discovered oxygen before Joseph Priestley, but Scheele published it later. Scheele's discoveries include chlorine, barium, molybdenum, tungsten and others.

Activity 3

To be demonstrated by the teacher

Aim: To prepare oxygen from hydrogen peroxide (H_2O_2) using manganese dioxide (MnO_2)

Materials required: H_2O_2, MnO_2, flat bottomed flask, dropping funnel, delivery tube, water trough, beehive shelf, two-holed rubber cork and gas jar

Procedure: The apparatus for the experiment is set up as shown in the figure given on the next page.

1. Some MnO_2 is taken in the flat-bottomed flask.

2. Using the dropping funnel, H_2O_2 is added drop by drop into the flask.

Observation: When H_2O_2 falls on MnO_2, it decomposes and releases oxygen gas, which can be seen as bubbles in the flask. This gas then passes through the delivery tube and gets collected in the inverted gas jar that is placed on the beehive shelf.

Conclusion: Oxygen gas, thus produced, displaces the water in the gas jar and gets collected in the empty space above the water. Since oxygen is not very soluble in water, it displaces water easily.

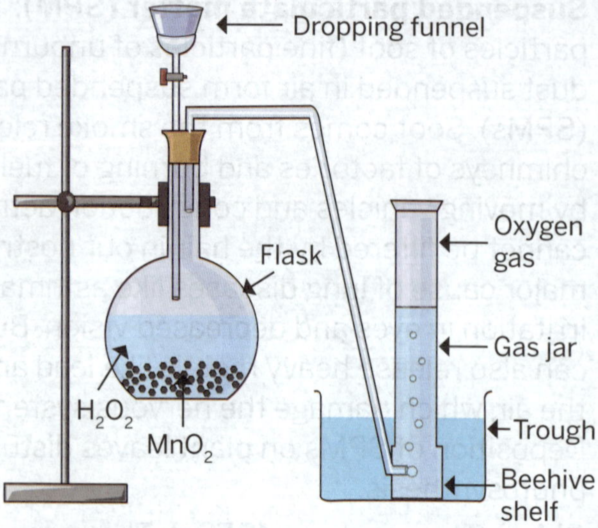

Science in Context

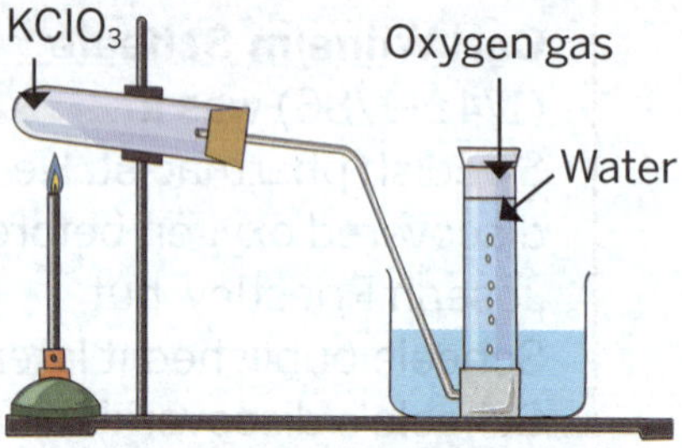

▲ Preparation of oxygen from potassium chlorate

Preparation of oxygen from potassium chlorate ($KClO_3$): When potassium chlorate is heated in the presence of the catalyst MnO_2, it decomposes into potassium chloride and oxygen.

$$2KClO_3 \xrightarrow{MnO_2} 2KCl + 3O_2$$

Note: Mostly, $KClO_3$ contains impurities like carbon which can be dangerous as it can explode during the reaction. Hence, it is usually not used in the preparation of oxygen in the laboratory.

Chemical Properties

Oxygen is highly reactive in nature. It reacts with metals, non-metals and many other compounds. Oxygen supports chemical reactions like rusting, combustion and oxidation.

Combustion

Oxygen is required for burning or combustion of fuels. Combustion is a chemical reaction that produces energy in the form of heat and light when a substance burns in the presence of oxygen. The energy produced during combustion is used to cook food, to run automobiles and various other purposes. Commonly used fuels are coal, wood, petrol, diesel, kerosene, CNG and LPG.

Rusting

It is the process of formation of a reddish-brown, flaky substance on the surface of iron objects in the presence of moisture (water vapour) and air (oxygen). This reddish-brown deposit formed on iron objects is known as rust. The presence of both water vapour and oxygen is necessary for the process of rusting to occur.

$$\text{Iron} + \text{Oxygen} + \text{Moisture} \longrightarrow \text{Hydrated iron or ferric oxide (rust)}$$

Oxidation

Oxygen reacts with other elements, such as metals and non-metals, to form their respective oxides. The chemical reaction in which there is addition of oxygen to form an oxide is called an **oxidation reaction**. Let us learn about the types of oxides formed with different elements

Let us learn about the types of oxides formed with different elements.

- With Metals: Oxygen reacts with metals to form basic oxides.

$$\text{Copper + Oxygen} \longrightarrow \text{Copper or cupric oxide}$$

- With Non-metals: Oxygen reacts with non-metals to form acidic oxides.

$$\text{Carbon + Oxygen} \longrightarrow \text{Carbon dioxide}$$

Oxidation reactions can be of three types: spontaneous, rapid and slow.

- **Spontaneous oxidation**: In this type of oxidation, a substance reacts immediately as soon as it comes in contact with oxygen. For example, sodium and potassium metals on exposure to air undergo spontaneous oxidation and burst into flames forming their respective oxides.
- **Rapid oxidation**: In this type of oxidation, a substance reacts with oxygen quickly releasing a lot of heat and light energy. For example, combustion of fuels like coal, petrol and LPG. Spontaneous oxidation is different from rapid oxidation as the former occurs on its own, while the latter occurs only if the substance is heated to its ignition temperature.
- **Slow oxidation**: In this type of oxidation, a substance reacts with oxygen very slowly over a long period of time. For example, rusting of iron and respiration.

Differences between some processes that require oxygen are listed in the following tables.

Respiration	Combustion
• This process takes place only in the living cells and under biological control. • Various enzymes are involved in this process. • This process takes place within the body temperature of the organism. • It is a slow process and the release of energy and the oxidation process of food take place in a step-wise order. • Nearly 40% of the energy that is liberated during this process is converted and stored as ATP (a form of chemical energy) & the 60% of the energy escapes in the form of body heat.	• This process won't take place in the living cells. • There is no involvement of enzymes in this process. • This process takes place at high temperature. • The release of energy takes place rapidly due to the spontaneous oxidation. • The energy is released in the form of light and heat. • Any substance that undergoes the process of combustion is referred as 'Fuel'

Combustion	Rusting
• This process takes place at high temperature. • It requires the presence of oxygen and an oxidation process. • Water will prevent the combustion • It is a very rapid process and takes minutes to occur • This process occurs in a variety of materials. • The heat will be released during this process in larger amount within a short period of time	• This process takes place at low temperature. • It requires the presence of oxygen and is an oxidation process. • Water is essential for rusting process. • It is a very slow process and takes few days of time. • This process occurs in the materials associated with iron. • The heat will be released during this process gradually in smaller amounts thus undetectable.

Revision Zone

Write T for True and F for False.

1. Carbon dioxide causes acid rain.
2. Oxygen reacts with non-metals to form basic oxides.
3. Respiration is an example of rapid oxidation.
4. Oxygen shows a characteristic taste.

Keywords

Air pollution: the introduction of harmful and undesirable substances in large amounts into the air as a result of human activities or natural processes

Combustion: a process that involves burning of a substance in the presence of oxygen with the release of heat and light energy

Ignition temperature: the minimum temperature at which a substance starts burning

Oxidation reaction: the chemical reaction that involves combining of oxygen with other elements to form an oxide

In a Nutshell

- Air consists of nitrogen (78 per cent), oxygen (21 per cent), and carbon dioxide, dust, smoke and other gases (1 per cent).
- Oxygen supports chemical reactions like rusting and combustion, and takes part in oxidation.
- During combustion, there is change in the mass of the products formed.
- Acid rain has adverse effects on our environment.
- Air quality in our atmosphere is disturbed due to various pollutants.

Exercise

1 Choose the correct answer for each of the following.

a. One of the major constituents of acid rain is

i. SPM ii. CFCs

iii. SO_2 iv. CO_2

b. Which of the following does not cause air pollution?

i. Flood ii. Wind erosion

iii. Forest fire iv. Volcanic eruption

c. Which of these helps in reducing air pollution?

i. Afforestation ii. Recycling wastes

iii. Use of CNG iv. All of these

d. Which of these is not a property of oxygen?

i. Supports combustion

ii. Colourless and odurless

iii. Sour in taste

iv. Can be liquefied

e. Which of these noble gases is used in the treatment of cancer?

i. Argon ii. Radon

iii. Helium iv. Krypton

2 Fill in the blanks.

a. Suspended particulate matter causes damage to the __________ (brain/lungs).

b. __________ (Oxygen/Nitrogen) supports combustion.

c. Food packaging cans are coated with __________ (silver/tin) to prevent rusting.

d. Addition of oxygen to elements to form oxides is called __________ (reduction/oxidation) reaction.

e. __________ (Argon/Helium) is filled in electric bulbs.

3 Write T for True and F for False.

a. Acid rain makes the soil rich in nutrients.

b. Magnesium burns in the presence of oxygen to form magnesium oxide.

c. Rusting takes place at a high temperature.

d. Combustion of fuels releases carbon dioxide and water.

e. In rapid oxidation, a substance reacts with oxygen very slowly over a long period of time.

4 Define the following terms.

a. Fuel

b. Combustion

c. Ignition temperature

d. Oxidation

e. Global warming

5 Differentiate between the following.

a. CFCs and SPMs

b. Painting and greasing

c. Rapid oxidation and slow oxidation

d. Respiration and combustion

e. Combustion and rusting

6 Answer the following questions in brief.

a. Explain the mass change that occur during burning of candle.

b. Write any two physical properties of oxygen.

c. Name the products obtained due to the combustion of biogas.

d. What is rust? Write the word equation involved in its formation.

e. Write the chemical equation for the formation of acid rain.

f. Write the word equations for the reaction of oxygen with any two metals and non-metals.

7 Answer the following questions in detail.

a. What are pollutants? How do these cause air pollution?

b. Write a note on composition of air.

c. What is rusting? How is it different from combustion?

d. Explain the process involved in formation of acid rain. Write the effects of acid rain.

e. Explain the change of mass involved during burning of magnesium.

f. Explain the different chemical properties of oxygen.

8 Think and answer.

What will happen if the percentage of oxygen is more than that of nitrogen in the atmosphere?
(Hint: Oxygen supports combustion.)

9 Project

Visit an industrial area in your locality and check how many industries have air filters in their chimneys. Prepare a report on it.

10 In the Library

a. You have learned about acid rain. Refer to books in your library to collect more information on its effect on Taj Mahal and prepare a report.

b. Smog is a combination of smoke and fog. In 1950, a new kind of smog called photochemical smog was described. Collect information on its definition, formation and effects on living things.

Worksheet

Subject Integration

a. Draw a pie chart to show the composition of air in a village that is surrounded by many trees and in an industrial area.

Village	Industrial Area

b. Does the composition of air remain the same in all places? If not, why is it so?

____

____

____

____

____

c. Do the constituents of air react with the other constituents?

____

____

____

____

Assessments

Assessment 1 (Chapters 1–4)

Maximum Marks: 40

1 Choose the correct answer for each of the following. (5 × 1 = 5)

a. Identify the Latin name for the element silver.
   i. *Aurum* ii. *Argentum* iii. *Hydrargyrum* iv. *Ferrum*

b. Which of these is the smallest particle that is found in a substance?
   i. Atom ii. Molecule iii. Compound iv. Mixture

c. Which of these is a physical change?
   i. Rusting of iron ii. Burning of paper iii. Folding of paper iv. Cooking of food

d. Identify the chemical formula of calcium hydroxide.
   i. CaOH ii. $Ca(OH)_2$ iii. Ca_2OH iv. $(Ca)_2OH$

e. Identify the characteristic of a chemical change.
   i. Change in both physical and chemical properties
   ii. No new products are formed
   iii. Temporary and reversible
   iv. Energy change is minimal

2 Fill in the blanks. (5 × 1 = 5)

a. The subatomic particles with a positive charge are called ________(protons/electrons).

b. The combining capacity of the atom of an element is known as its ________ (atomicity/valency).

c. ________ (Solids/Gases) neither have a definite shape nor a definite volume.

d. Soil erosion is an example of ________ (desirable change/undesirable change).

e. Suspension is an example of a ________ (homogeneous/heterogeneous) mixture.

3 Write T for True and F for False. (5 × 1 = 5)

a. Atom is the smallest unit of matter.

b. During a chemical change, minimum amount of energy is absorbed or released.

c. Intermolecular space is same in solids, liquids and gases.

d. Boiling of water is an example of reversible change.

e. An emulsion is a mixture of two or more immiscible liquids.

4 Give reasons for the following. (5 × 2 = 10)

a. Some elements exhibit variable valency.

b. Rotting of fruits is a chemical change.

c. Solids have fixed shape.

d. Air is a homogeneous mixture.

e. The electrons do not contribute to the mass of the atom.

5 Answer the following questions. (5 × 3 = 15)

a. Mention the characteristic features of compounds.

b. What is paper chromatography and explain its principle.

c. Explain with the help of an activity that matter occupies space.

d. Explain the structure of an atom with a diagram.

e. Explain how immiscible liquids are separated using a separating funnel.

Assessment 2 (Chapters 5–7) **Maximum Marks: 40**

1 Choose the correct answer for each of the following. (5 × 1 = 5)

a. Which of these is a balanced chemical equation?

i. $2Mg + 2O_2 \rightarrow 2MgO$ ii. $Fe + S \rightarrow FeS$

iii. $2H_2O \rightarrow 2H_2 + 2O_2$ iv. $Hg + O_2 \rightarrow HgO$

b. When a test tube containing ammonium chloride is heated carefully over a Bunsen burner, it releases a ________.

i. Pungent odour ii. Fruity odour iii. Flowery odour iv. Pleasant odour

c. The non-metal that is a good conductor of electricity is

i. Chlorine ii. Nitrogen iii. Graphite iv. Oxygen

d. Which of the following metal is not ductile in nature?

i. Copper ii. Aluminium iii. Silver iv. Potassium

e. One of the major constituents of acid rain is

i. SPM ii. CFCs iii. SO_2 iv. CO_2

2 Fill in the blanks. (5 × 1 = 5)

a. $2KClO_3 \rightarrow 2$ ________ (KCl/K_2O) + $3O_2$.

b. The new substances formed during a chemical reaction are known as ________ (products/reactants).

c. The property by which metals can be beaten into thin sheets is called ________ (sonority/malleability).

d. Global warming is caused by ________ gas (carbon dioxide/oxygen).

e. The percent of ________ gas is 21% in the atmosphere (nitrogen/oxygen).

3 Write T for True and F for False. (5 × 1 = 5)

a. Diamond is used to cut hard metals and rocks.

b. In a chemical equation, the products are written on the right-hand side.

c. Precipitate is the insoluble solid formed as product during some chemical reactions.

d. Metals are non-sonorous.

e. Carbon dioxide causes acid rain.

4 Give reasons for the following. (5 × 2 = 10)

a. Chemical reactions involve a change of energy during the course of the reaction.

b. Combustion of coal is an example of rapid oxidation.

c. Chlorofluorocarbons are responsible for ozone hole.

d. Argon gas is filled in electric bulbs.

e. Iron pipes used for supplying water to our homes are galvanized.

5 Answer the following questions. (5 × 3 = 15)

a. Explain the formation and harmful effects of acid rain.

b. List the significance of a balanced chemical equation.

c. Describe the properties and uses of any two metalloids.

d. Write a note on chemical equations that involves energy. Give examples for each.

e. Compare the general properties of metals and non-metals.

NOTES